A Practical Guide *to* Becoming a Composer

A wealth of advice, tips, strategies, and examples

Arthur J. Michaels

© 2020 Arthur J. Michaels
All Rights Reserved.

ISBN: 9798643906278

To all composers and those who want to be composers

Nothing in the world can take the place of persistence. Talent will not; nothing is more common than unsuccessful men of talent. Genius will not; the world is full of educated derelicts. Persistence and determination alone are omnipotent.

—*Calvin Coolidge, 30th President of the United States*

Table of Contents

Acknowledgements 11
Introduction 13
I. Tapping Your Talent 20
    1. Be ready for inspiration. 21
    2. Understand your creative process. 24
    3. Recognize that on first attempts creative works don't often come out in perfect form with little revision necessary. ..35
    4. Overcome procrastination. 39
    5. Let experience and practice help you identify your artistic style, musical strengths, and composing preferences... 46
    6. Identify your strengths and weaknesses. 51
    7. Seek feedback and constructive criticism on your work. 56
    8. Conquer not being good enough. 60
    9. Tame your internal editing, critical mind. 62
    10. Recognize a mentor if one appears, and tap your mentor's knowledge and skills. 66
    11. Take courses locally and online. 70
    12. Experiment with musical, stylistic, and orchestration techniques. 71
    13. Organize your work and stay organized. 74
    14. Keep track of your contacts. 77
II. Becoming More Educated and Skilled With or Without Formal Music Composition Training 82
    1. Be patient and persistent. 83

2. Start and stay mainly with what is most familiar. 84
3. Learn music theory. 87
4. Consider the music composition curricula of colleges. 90
5. Study music history. 91
6. Study—and play—the instruments and
   styles for which you want to compose. 92
7. Play in (or conduct) a community, college, or high school
   band or orchestra; sing in (or conduct) a community or
   church choir; or create your own ensemble. 93
8. Offer instruction on your primary instrument. 94
9. Volunteer your services in your community. 96
10. Become more familiar with music's unfamiliar aspects. 98
11. Get a private teacher, locally for
    one-on-one learning, or online. 99
12. Engage in an internship or apprenticeship. 101
13. Listen to and analyze a lot of music—especially
    the kind of material you want to create. 102
14. Pursue opportunities that appear. 104
15. Ask, ask, ask. 105
16. Equip yourself with the tools of the trade. 107
17. Ensure your work's professional appearance. 111
18. Manage your time for your greatest advantage. 116
19. Set goals and measure progress. 121
20. Take local college courses (or audit them),
    adult school classes, summer school offerings,
    and community enrichment programs. 123
21. Get a library card. 124
22. Gather a reference library. 125
23. Attend live concerts of the kinds of music you compose. 129
24. Join a performing rights society. 130
25. Join professional organizations and internet
    forums, and attend conferences. 131

26. Network effectively. 133
27. Apply conference skills. 136
28. Promote yourself on social media and get your
    works performed, published, viewed, or purchased. 138
29. Create a website to increase your
    exposure and sell your music. 144
30. Build a YouTube channel...145
31. Start a blog. 151
32. Study the market...152
33. How to submit music for publication consideration. 155
34. Enter contests and competitions. 161
35. Prepare for rejection and use it to your advantage. 163
36. Study the publishing contract. 167
37. Self-publish your music. 170
38. Be thoroughly professional in your dealings with everyone....173
39. Seek commissions. 178
40. Check resources often because they change. 179
41. Practice, practice, practice...180
42. Take a wider view. 181
43. Trust the process of learning these skills, of
    becoming increasingly more adept at composing, of
    becoming more prolific, and of promoting your work. 183

Resources 184
Contributors..195
Index 209

Acknowledgements

A small amount of dread always accompanies my pursuing a creative project like writing a book or composing music. No wonder with such vulnerability I'm so relieved at the end of these processes! When I complete a major job, I am also grateful to the many people who helped me in a work's often complex course; who put up with my occasional moodiness, crankiness, and aloofness as I grappled with a project's content and direction; who shared in my joyful, exultant cries celebrating small and large milestones in finishing major tasks; and who otherwise contributed, large and small, to my work.

I am grateful to many people for their help in my writing this book. This work took about three years to complete—about six years, actually, if you include the planning. To my surprise, those I need to thank for their help in writing this book date back much further than just those six years.

Thank you to:

- My parents, for nurturing both the music and the writing in me, and for instilling in me a love of learning.
- My spouse, Cathy, for her suggestions, critique, comments, and patience.
- Professors at the Eastman School of Music who encouraged me and believed in me long before I believed in myself.

- My mentors, Everett Gates at Eastman, chair of the music education department, and Lou Bynum, my first boss in a real job (teaching), for their encouragement, guidance, and support.
- Publishers of my music, articles, books, and photographs.
- This book's 24 contributors. Because of their varied backgrounds and experiences, including their comments was enlightening and inspirational: Composers Ronald J. Brown, Raymond Burkhart, Chris Carlone, Kim Diehnelt, Paolo Fradiani, Divan Gattamorta, Mike Hall, Grahame Gordon Innes, R. Duane Hendricks, Zander Hulme, Pamela Illanes-Tatsuoka, Laurie Jeanne Crockett, Glenn Martin, Michael J. Miller, Teresa O'Connell, Laura Pettigrew, Elizabeth Raum, Ari Romppanen, Alex Shapiro, Mark Taylor, Tony Tester, Jukka Viitasaari, Sahlia Wong, and Rain Worthington. See their biographical information in the "Contributors" section.

Arthur J. Michaels
July 2020

Introduction

I went to college and graduate school, preparing for a career in music education. I have never taken a composition course, yet today I am an award-winning composer. The music composition skills I've acquired came from learning outside the classroom during the last 40+ years.

I've filled this book with the lessons and practical ideas I've learned over the years—lessons and advice that don't often appear in music composition curricula. These practices include indispensable, detailed how-to information that I and other composers have garnered through years of experience. Thus, this book is a roadmap to becoming a better composer, to advancing one's skills, and, as part of that process, to increasing one's creative flow, with or without a formal education.

Anyone from the junior high school level through the college years who wants to pursue composing can use these ideas to be more skilled and more prolific. Anyone who wants to increase one's activity and output in composing as part of an allied field, as I did, can also gain much from applying these skills and advice. Anyone who is already studying to be a composer or who is eyeing a career change to composing could also benefit from applying these lessons.

Established composers can also use this book to sharpen their skills and acquire new abilities. Anyone else who wishes to become a composer—hobbyist or professional—can greatly benefit from applying this book's ideas. However, in this book I assume that aspiring composers have at least basic musical knowledge and at least some training on any instrument.

Although I've never taken a composing course, my training as an instrumental music teacher facilitated my becoming a published composer. Having been taught to play band and orchestra instruments and teaching instrumental music inspired much of my composing, as it still does. To become an instrumental music teacher, I took lessons on all the band and stringed instruments. I was a saxophone and clarinet major, and I had taught myself to play piano, guitar, and flute in high school, so I had a head start learning to play some instruments. When I graduated from college in 1970, I became a public school band director in grades 4-12. My first published piece was a saxophone quartet called "Danzonetta," which I wrote at age 28, in 1976, for an ensemble of my high school students.

Even though I've been composing since I was 12, I very much regret overlooking opportunities to learn and grow as a composer during all of my schooling. In high school, college, and graduate school, I wanted to be a more knowledgeable, prolific composer, but the composer in me was, well, lost. Even though I began to learn and apply many of the ideas in this book since I was in college, I didn't have adequate direction to best ensure my learning and progress as a composer. Furthermore, I didn't understand which steps to take to improve my composing skills and increase my productivity, and I didn't know how to commence that journey. I didn't know who to ask for help, and I didn't know what to ask of those who may have helped me.

In retrospect, I believed the myth that all composers just "know" how to compose, with no guidance or training, and that great music just mysteriously "comes" to all composers. Silly notion, isn't it? Composing is an art that requires study and practice. If I had been more aware of the ideas in this book, I would have been much better able to guide myself to seek a more formal approach to composing. I would also have readily taken the excellent advice of those who offered guidance (See item 14 in Section II).

I began clarifying and articulating the ideas in this book a few years ago. Subtitled *A wealth of advice, tips, strategies, and examples,* this book helps composers advance their skills and increase their creative flow with or without the benefit of classroom learning. Had I been able to apply these lessons when I didn't know what I didn't know, I would have taken far fewer composer missteps during the last few decades. Armed with these lessons, I would also have been better able to navigate a course to greater productivity, and I would have been better equipped to keep stoking my creative fires. I would have taken composition courses as a college undergraduate or in graduate school.

I was fortunate that my parents were both educators and college music minors, so they could readily guide me to the teaching career I pursued. But they could not guide me toward composing opportunities as effectively because they, too, didn't know what they didn't know. If this book had been available when I was growing up, my parents would surely have bought it. This book could have helped them steer me more toward a composing career, if at the time I had expressed interest in that pursuit.

If this book had been available when I decided to improve my skills as a composer, I would also have bought it. Even now, as a published, award-winning composer, if I saw this book, I'd buy it. That's because earning a high school diploma, a college degree, or even an advanced degree is a wonderful, promising accomplishment—I know. I did that. But diplomas and degrees don't guarantee that you know how to advance your skills and increase your productivity and success. They also don't ensure your continued success in today's complicated, competitive business world. Furthermore, the idea that a degree doesn't necessarily guarantee success is especially true when you make major or even minor career changes.

This book focuses on two main areas: Bringing out, summoning, and tapping one's talent; and becoming more educated and skilled with or without formal education in music composition. Both main ideas are vital because the skills explained in "Tapping Your Talent," the first section, work concurrently with the ideas in "Becoming More Educated and Skilled With or Without Formal Music Composition Training," the second section. That's why in the first section I refer to items in the second section, and vice versa.

Because composing music is so varied with an enormous number of opportunities, a diverse, international group of 24 fellow composers augments this book's ideas. Most of these composers come from backgrounds different from mine, and they work in different genres and styles. Their biographical information appears in the Resources section.

This book's specifics and comprehensiveness make it an indispensable reference that you read, reread, and consult often. I must stress that you can benefit from applying this book's ideas with or without the benefit of formal training in music composition. In fact, the internet, YouTube, and many other online resources blur the lines between formal education and informal learning. Thus, this book is both a necessary standalone guide for composers outside of formal learning spheres and a vital supplement for composers who are studying or who have studied in formal learning circles.

In addition, because this book includes details of specific composer how-to skills, composers and those who want to be composers get an intimate, unique view of the private professional procedures and practices of fellow composers—a perspective few composers ever see.

I make no judgments on whether formal education in music composition is better than an informal approach, or whether an informal pursuit is better than formal study. Fact is, if "formal" education includes any classroom setting and "informal" education includes any learning outside of that setting, then "formally" trained composers actually learn in both settings.

I present these ideas and skills mostly in a loosely logical order. I say "loosely logical order" because as an adjunct to one item I often suggest reading other closely related items elsewhere in the book. In addition, the ideas in which you are already practiced can serve as review. Reading them and rereading them can help you enhance your composing and gain greater insight to propel your moving forward on your creative path. Reading these ideas and rereading them can also suggest course adjustments to skills you already possess—doing something slightly differently, perhaps. Considering all the ideas in this book, you'll want to focus on the ideas and skills that draw your attention the most.

Volumes have been written about each idea in this book. However, my purpose in this book is to encapsulate the information and skills and present them in terse, practical terms in a single source. If a topic especially captures your attention and interest, that topic can serve as a springboard to further enrichment. I've listed many sources for supplementary reading and pursuit in the Resources section.

Some composers will look at this book's content and think that I am completely wrong. For them, I probably am wrong! So I want to point out—and stress—that the ideas in this book describe mainly my path as a composer, and that my path isn't necessarily

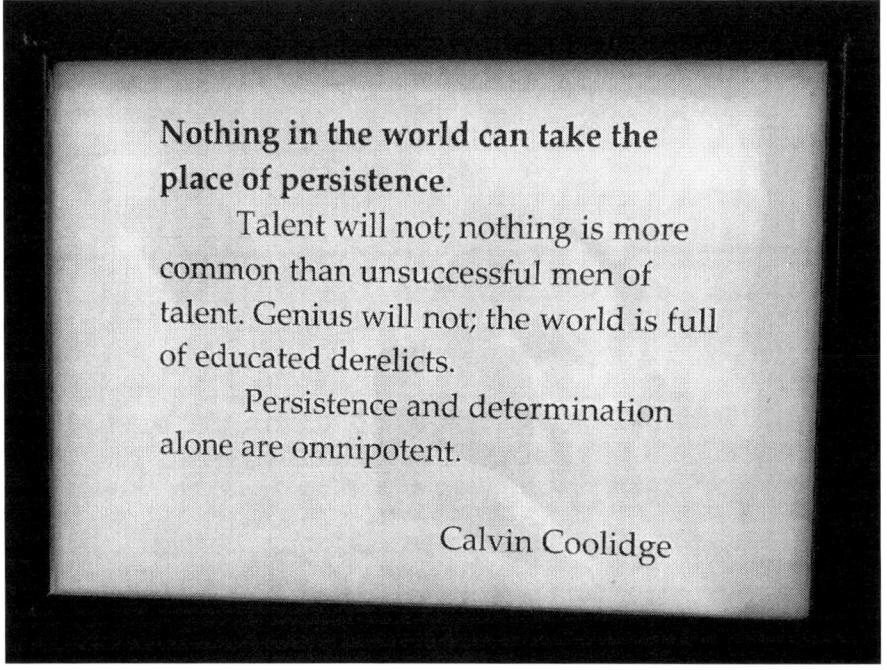

Nothing in the world can take the place of persistence.

Talent will not; nothing is more common than unsuccessful men of talent. Genius will not; the world is full of educated derelicts.

Persistence and determination alone are omnipotent.

Calvin Coolidge

the "right" path for you. Over the years, I've mostly followed a traditional path to publication. In my experience, ironically, getting published doesn't always mean that one's music will be widely performed. Today's publishing and composing climate invites—no, demands—many different paths to one's successful career as a composer. I delve deeper into this idea in item #42, "Take a Wider View," in the book's second section.

The information, ideas, and skills in this book also apply to those who aspire to write, paint, draw, work with digital art or mixed media, photograph, sculpt, create pottery, and work in arts and crafts. This book can also energize and increase the creativity of those in business and in the sciences. In fact, anyone with a creative bent can benefit from acting on this book's advice and applying this book's lessons to other creative pursuits.

Let this book's guidance, insights, and suggestions inspire you and crystalize the lessons within you so that you can apply them in your endeavors. While you read this book, keep the book's epigraph in mind. Let the epigraph guide your creative journey, as it has guided and continues to guide mine—I have its words displayed prominently in my office. Dig in, and watch your skills, productivity, and success blossom!

Tapping Your Talent

1 Be ready for inspiration.

I've discovered that I never know when inspiration will strike, so to be prepared when my creativity flows, I stash music manuscript paper everywhere—in the night stand by my bed, in my car, at my desk, in my suitcase when I travel, and even in my pocket with a pencil when I exercise. It isn't uncommon for me to pull over to the side of the road to jot down a musical idea. My wife never acts surprised when I suddenly pull off the road, retrieve paper, and begin writing—she knows what I'm doing.

These days I more often sing music ideas and record accompanying notes into my iPhone's voice memos feature than write them down with paper and pencil. When I'm working at my desk, I use the app Simple Recording, or because it's convenient, I bring up Finale and enter my idea into a new document. I also have a Finale file of these kinds of ideas, so I also bring up that file and enter new material there.

You'll find many smart phone and computer apps for writing music, but for my iPhone I find them more hindering than helpful, so I stick to manuscript paper, entering musical ideas right into

Finale, or singing into my iPhone and computer for transcription later.

U.S.-based film composer Mike Hall's strategy for preparedness is similar to mine. "For me, usually the time I get a riff or melody in my head is usually at the most inconvenient moments, like driving, so I prefer to have a voice recorder of some kind ready to hum the idea with maybe some ideas to go with it," he says. "I use a small, inexpensive, hand-held Olympus digital recorder to get down my ideas."

Canadian composer R. Duane Hendricks says, "I put almost all of my ideas on staff paper in pencil. Most often I write before I play, not wanting my instrumental technique to get in the way, putting my skills and my limitations into the mix."

U.K.-based composer Grahame Gordon Innes says, "Sometimes I sketch on paper but not always. It depends on the complexity of my ideas. Pre-1998, I did everything on manuscript paper up to and including full scores. In 1998, I got Finale and started transcribing my then completed scores accordingly. Since then I have written and sketched less on paper, keeping more and more details in my mind and incorporating them as I work through full scores in Finale."

Brazilian composer Divan Gattamorta initially writes ideas in notebooks or on staff paper. He then notates these ideas in Pro Tools.

U.S.-based composer Pamela Illanes-Tatsuoka says, "I write down my ideas, even if they are not fully developed, and I usually come back to these ideas later. Sometimes two to three melodies are in my head at the same time, so I try to write these down or record them so that I don't forget them."

U.S.-based composer Laurie Jeanne Crockett says, "I'm old school and I like hard copy, so when composing, I reach for staff paper and a sharpened pencil. Occasionally I've had a melody come to me in my car and I've then sung it into my phone."

Canadian composer Ronald J. Brown says, "I sometimes scribble ideas for a composition on a piece of scrap paper. It could be a rhythmic pattern or a melodic fragment. I'm not really organized in my approach. Generally, I'll have an idea I want to explore. I'll then open a blank score in Finale and start writing it down. As soon as I do that, it starts to change. I'll follow an idea to see where it wants to go. Sometimes I'll write 50-60 measures before I decide it is or is not worth pursuing; sometimes I can tell after only 4-8 measures that the idea will not sustain itself."

U.S.-based composer Christopher Carlone's preparedness is different. "My DAW (digital audio workstation) scratch pad is where my ideas are born," he says. "To someone who needs to write many minutes of music and on tight deadlines for YouTube creators, I find that my ideas spill out faster than I can notate. It saves time by getting my basic chord structure and melody down on a lead sheet and orchestrating from there. Only when I work on feature films, where motifs need to develop throughout, do I use traditional notation software like Sibelius or Finale."

U.K.-based composer Tony Tester also most often relies on his DAW. "If I'm in my studio, I quickly record ideas using the DAW I consider suitable for the piece," he says. "I use Cubase if it's classical or jazz; Reason if it's a more contemporary piece, dance, dubstep, or hiphop; and Logic for most anything else. If I do not have access to a keyboard, workstation, or smartphone, I happily go old school and jot down ideas on a piece of paper, a serviette [napkin], or whatever else is convenient."

2 Understand your creative process.

To understand your creative process, first become familiar with your work habits. The creative process and one's work habits are closely connected because one affects the other. Staying familiar with your work habits is also important because work habits can change. For me, for example, writing down descriptive notes on musical ideas and notating all that I conjure right away are vital parts of my capturing the mood, style, instrumentation, and interpretation of an initial idea. These first steps in my creative process help me more fully develop an idea as more of it appears.

In addition, becoming more aware of my creative process and my work habits has let me make changes to my work habits that help me increase both productivity and the flow of creative ideas. For example, carrying manuscript paper everywhere lets me capture ideas that I might otherwise lose. The same boost in productivity occurred when I began singing ideas into my iPhone's voice memos app. These changes—adaptations—to my work habits reveal the vital connection between understanding one's creative process and becoming familiar with one's work habits.

Summoning inspiration

There is huge variation among composers in their creative triggers and in their creative processes. For this reason, become aware of your creative process, examine its steps, and make beneficial adaptations and changes to it for increasing your flow of ideas and productivity.

Composer Laurie Jeanne Crockett draws inspiration from internal sources and external sources. "My internal source of inspiration is my religious faith," she says. "Philippians 4:8 is a verse to which I aspire because it admonishes one to think about things that are honest and just and lovely. I write sacred music as well as instrumental pieces because at a very deep level I feel compelled to write songs about the God I love and worship. I think, whatever your world view, it can't help but influence your music, and end up being, in some part, the source from which you draw inspiration. The external sources are forces that come at you while you're living your life that affect you emotionally; i.e., a visit with a good friend, a beautiful sunset, a walk in the woods, a break-up, death of a loved one, etc. The emotional responses to these events produce a compelling need to share that experience through music. It's a very powerful medium to create a common bond between people because they're emotions we all share and events to which we can all relate."

Composer Laurie Jeanne Crockett's creative process includes improvisation to beckon inspiration. "I most often start on the piano with a melodic riff in the right hand that I stumble upon by just improvising a bit," she says. "Sometimes lyrics in my head generate their own rhythm and melody. I'll play the section over several times until I memorize it. Then I quickly write the notes (sometimes just the note heads) on the staff paper and later go back and add stems, chords, and left hand. Then, as I play through my new little bit of song, I listen to where it wants to go next and jot it down in the same fashion."

U.S.-based composer Rain Worthington takes a comprehensive view of inspiration. "My inspirations come from everyday living, emotions, and experiences," she says. "Composing for me is a process of translating or channeling life into music. Inspirations can be triggered through the sounds of trucks backing up, the wind in the trees, rhythms of walking, or the lingering images or feelings of dreams. The most important thing for me is to allow enough silent space in my everyday life to absorb these sounds of life and then begin to hear the personal translations of the sounds as they emerge as music."

Australian game audio designer Zander Hulme's inspiration takes time. "I know some composers who can write very quickly, but for me, most any work worth writing home about takes time," he says. "I once co-wrote a stage musical with another composer and we would have weekly one-hour writing sessions together. He would do some improvising, and by the end of the hour he would have written most of a song. I would take it away, and come back the next week with an arrangement of his song along with a draft of my own."

Composer Mike Hall derives inspiration from emotions. "When I am searching for inspiration," he says, "I find those things that invoke the most emotion. Whatever that emotion is usually tends to jar loose my creative juices. I also listen to music in the style or mood I am looking to create. Sometimes I will talk with other artist friends of mine and bounce ideas off of them."

U.S.-based composer Glenn Martin says, "My biggest inspiration is to have a commission and a deadline to meet. Then I picture the group sitting on stage and singing or playing my piece. That gets me excited and ideas start flowing."

Composer R. Duane Hendricks thinks similarly. "Commissions inspire me. Deadlines inspire me. Impending performances inspire me," he says. "The questions 'what if?' 'what's next?,' 'can I…?' inspire me. Frequently I go to bed telling myself that an idea, or the solution to a problem, or the answers to 'what next?' and 'now what?' will appear when it is time. They always do."

"When I am composing for a junior high school or senior high school group," Hendricks says, "I often read fantasy books, which are aimed at those ages. A character or situation will often lead to a musical theme, a musical feel, or a specific instrument or instrumental combination."

U.K.-based composer Grahame Gordon Innes says, "My inspiration comes from Scandinavia, Russia, Ukraine, history, world peace, personal feelings, nature, mythology, the sea, the great composers, astronomy, and science fiction. My works usually describe at least one topic in these groups."

Italian composer Paolo Fradiani's creative output includes reading books to gain inspiration. "My becoming inspired isn't the same for each composition," he says. "However, reading books stirs my creativity. For instance, I've been inspired by reading *Temperament*, by Stuart Isacoff, Plato's *Timaeus*, and Aristotle's *Metaphysics*. My orchestra piece "Archetypi," which concerns geometry, math, and philosophy, was inspired by my reading the works of Heraclitus."

U.S.-based composer Michael J. Miller's creative process includes, surprisingly, disengaging. "My writing process involves working out ideas on a midi keyboard (Native Instruments' Komplete Kontrol S61)," he says, "and then inputting them with notation software. I am a firm believer that our minds continue working things out when we're disengaged, so sometimes I'll purposely leave a project for a few hours, even days, before returning to the keyboard or computer. Sometimes, not always, ideas present themselves this way more clearly than I could have ever imagined."

Miller's inspiration comes from many sources. "Places inspire me," he says. "People inspire me. Experiences inspire me. The composer who never leaves his or her comfort zone (house, hometown, etc.) is at a severe disadvantage compared to the composer who travels, meets new people, eats great food, and experiences the diversity that exists in the world. Listening to great music—including that of current composers—also inspires me."

Composer Christopher Carlone says, "Inspiration is tricky for the media composer. Creators I work with often use temporary tracks that can either provide huge inspiration or leave the creative process completely stifled. When I write background music for YouTubers, however, I find that there are few people from whom I can draw inspiration because media composing is a relatively new outlet for composing. I am able to draw the most inspiration from the project itself and less from listening to other music. Thus, I try to avoid temporary tracks so that I can allow myself a clean slate on projects."

Understanding your own creative process and how you summon inspiration can pay big dividends when considering commissions and potential clients. "I know my creative process well enough to know how vital timing is when game developers seek my services," says composer Zander Hulme. "I'm often approached near the end of a project and asked to provide all of the music that the game requires. This is not when I do my best work. There must be a balance. If I'm contracted early enough, there is time for my ideas to percolate and time to get immersed in the game design and its art. I grasp the visceral feeling of playing the game. I can then take away these feelings and iterate them many times, refining and honing the music so that it truly fits the project. On the other hand, if I'm contracted too early, the developers sometimes don't really know what they want from their game aesthetically, and I then have to waste time with a splatter-gun approach until I find something that sticks."

Finally, U.K.-based composer Tony Tester says, "I don't know why, and I do not wish to sound smug, but luckily I have never struggled to find inspiration. I have always found the creative process to be easy. When writing jingles and educational songs, ideas almost always comes from the concept of the piece or its title. Whether I'm writing a jingle for an airline company or an educational song about brushing your teeth, the subject matter defines the outline of the melody and harmony, and these qualities then influence the arrangement. The melody, harmony, and orchestration are cut and woven together from the same cloth. For me, everything naturally falls into place from the moment of musical conception."

After inspiration

After capturing my initial inspiration, transcribing my singing from apps to my music notation software is most often the next step in my creative process. Transcription comes easily to me. If transcription isn't your forte and you can learn how to use apps quickly, a smart phone music notation app might be your most convenient and productive choice (see the "Resources" section for music notation product suggestions).

In addition to melodies and other music motifs, I often write or record notes on the instrumentation and other musical elements I'm hearing, including playing instructions, tempo markings, instrumentation, and other designations and textures. These embellishments let me recapture and develop the spirit of my initial inspiration when I'm at the computer. I try to be as specific and as detailed in these accompanying notes as I can be because without these details I sometimes lose the essence of the musical idea.

Sometimes I record or notate a new musical idea, and nothing more about the idea comes to me. Then the idea just waits in my files for more inspiration and action. More often, though, the process of embellishing my initial ideas and notes continues. After I write down or record an original idea, I hear it repeatedly in my mind for a few minutes, sometimes for hours, and if I conjure up sufficient revisions and accompanying new material, I then sing these ideas into my iPhone and record more notes with as much detail as I can in that moment.

I don't force repeatedly going over the idea. I've learned that it's just my internal signal that there's more there. I then notate the idea into Finale. I often continue to revise and add to the idea when I enter it into Finale. When I embellish a new idea, I often arrive at the point at which I know the instrumentation I plan to apply to the idea—concert band, strings, an ensemble, chorus, for example. So my enhanced sketch then takes shape in a full-fledged score. And voilà! I've begun a new work in Finale!

Most of the musical ideas I create need to simmer. I write down ideas as they come, but I often sing and play them in my mind for days, weeks, months, and even years before I develop them.

Consider "Seophonic Rhapsody," for the Lycoming College Concert Band, a commissioned work that I undertook in 2009. The piece consists of two contrasting sections. The first part is slow and legato. The second section is faster and staccato. I wrote the main theme of the first part in the car on my way home from the college after meeting with the band director—I was so inspired! I had created the second part's main motif several years before. It had just waited in my files as an undeveloped theme until I realized it was the perfect fit for this piece's contrasting second part. "Seophonic Rhapsody" is published by Aamano Music, where you can hear this piece.

One exception in particular stands out in my generally slow creative process. A few years ago, the main theme of my wind ensemble piece "Mockingbirds" came to me during a neighborhood walk. The local mockingbirds sang the melody to me (really, they did!), and I sang it into my iPhone. When I returned home I began work on the piece, and I was so inspired that within two weeks, I completed "Mockingbirds," a moderately difficult piece with a duration of about 2:50. Two weeks from idea to completed work is lightning-fast composing speed for me. This work is also published by Aamano Music.

My creative process has extremes, too. In 1973 I composed two SATB (soprano, alto, tenor, bass) a cappella settings of parts of the traditional Catholic mass, "Agnus Dei" and "Sanctus."

After completing these pieces, I stored them in a drawer, literally, for 30 years. Around 2003, I retrieved both manuscripts and entered them into Finale. Then, sporadically during the next 10 years or so, I reworked both pieces, changing the music here and there, adding and removing some sections, and cleaning up the notation. "Agnus Dei" is published by Holysheetmusic.com, and "Sanctus" is published by Choralife.com.

When I reviewed these pieces after 30 years, I reworked them in light of my growth as a composer. I believe my evolution as a composer contributed to my wanting to revise these pieces. Your own artistic growth could trigger your amending projects you completed many years ago, so be aware of this possibility as you consider your creative process. In fact, if you don't do so already, you might want to make periodic reviews of your older works a part of your routine. I do so often.

The process of my developing a musical idea is similar to the process of my thinking it up. I mull over an initial idea often for days, asking myself where I "hear" this idea going, and with which instruments do I hear it. After I've decided the instrumentation or ensemble makeup and entered the idea into Finale, I then try adding more to the idea, and if I like that direction, I continue with it. If not, I sometimes delete what I had sketched (or most often save it for possible use elsewhere) and try again, perhaps with a different ensemble or instrumentation. I might try a different key signature, placing the melody with different instruments from my initial choice. I might also change the melody and key signature to suit certain instrument ranges better, thus changing a line's color.

Another part of my creative process I've recognized is that I most often work on several projects at once. For instance, simultaneously I may be composing a woodwind quintet, a choral piece, and a concert band piece; proofreading parts to a concert band piece; revising conductor and rehearsal notes to yet a different concert band piece; reworking a piece I wrote decades ago; and preparing a submission to one or several publishers. Ironically, I never feel bogged down or overwhelmed working this way. In fact, working on many projects at the same time keeps my mood bright and my outlook optimistic. It ultimately inspires my working diligently and keeps me productive and looking ahead.

Because I work on several projects at once, I keep a log in my iMac's Stickies app with the name of each piece I'm working on, the history of the tasks I've completed on the work, and its current status. I use Stickies as a to-do list. When I stop working on a piece for several weeks, for instance, my Stickies notes let me take up the project again without losing my place in its progress to completion. I also add tasks to these notes as I think of them. Using Stickies is quick and efficient. These ideas are related to setting goals and establishing to-do lists. See item #19, "Set goals and measure progress," in the next section.

The description a few paragraphs above on how some of my ideas become full-fledged compositions shows that I'm aware of this aspect of my creative process. Acquiring a fuller awareness of your own creative workings can help you know how to encourage ideas to flow, when your ideas appear, how to take advantage of these times, and how to increase these opportunities. Study your own creative process. Understand it. Becoming aware of and understanding your own creative activity can inspire you and, ultimately, increase your creativity and productivity.

Titles

Part of my creative process often includes brainstorming titles. I try to create the catchiest, most effective titles that capture the essence of the ideas I'm creating. Finale, my music notation software, doesn't have a sticky note feature, so to this end, I often add text notes on proposed titles into the music. Titles come to me in the same ways as do musical ideas. I keep all of these ideas. When I think I've exhausted coming up with title choices, I begin evaluating them, editing them, and paring them down to a final choice.

I take titling my works seriously. A work title is like a magazine cover—it's designed to match the subject, and its purpose is to get the reader to look at what's inside. Thus, crafty, catchy, bright, and appropriate titles of musical works lure publishers and conductors to open your score and look. In addition, creating such titles inspires me!

I most often compose the music before or while I am thinking up its title. However, my conjuring up plays on words occasionally sparks a catchy title without having composed the music yet. To this end, I'll create the title and then compose the music to fit the title. My easy concert band piece "First Foray in Five-Four" is such an example. The title came to me weeks before I began composing the piece. The title "Tampering with Tempi from Tempe to Tampa" came to me months before I composed the concert band work of that title.

Here are some of the other titles that have worked for me: "Bluesy Chalumeau Cha-Cha" (concert band), "Jazzy Capriccio" (concert band), "Euphotrombotonia" (concert band"), and "Two Trillion Triplets" (brass quintet). If you were a band director or a publisher, wouldn't these titles at least get you to open the scores and look?

3 Recognize that on first attempts creative works don't often come out in perfect form with little revision necessary.

Composing music is an art. Its creations require diligent honing and revision. For this reason, the creative process is a path lined with uncertainty, and it is filled with wrong turns and "mistakes," and initially creating what seem to be disjointed bits and pieces. By saving writing and musical fragments and ideas, you don't let what sometimes seems to be a hodgepodge stymie your continuing with an idea.

I must clarify "mistakes." I believe there really aren't any. If a musical passage doesn't work in one piece, it may work in another piece. I save all my musical inspirations and every work's iterations for this reason.

Create a file scheme for your work that makes sense to you. Mine is simple. I save my musical ideas by title, if a title is part of the initial idea, or simply "new" with the month, day, and year ("mm-dd-yynew"). I organize my writing ideas by the name or keyword with the same date format. Periodically I review these undeveloped ideas to see if anything new comes to mind, and I then decide if I should expand the idea into a project. Read more on file systems in item #13.

Don't think of reviewing a wealth of undeveloped ideas as daunting and discouraging. In fact, I find this process exhilarating because I often continue with works that I had previously set aside. Don't let dry spells, dead ends, fragments, and "mistakes" get you down. Each dry spell, dead end, and "mistake" brings you closer to finishing a work.

To insulate myself from worrying about mistakes and dead ends, and to encourage myself about this part of my creative process, I've hung a sign over my desk that reminds me of my "Six Ps of Creativity." Here are the sign contents and their meaning to me:

- **Power.** Power is enabling your creativity to blossom and grow, even while knowing that others are more skilled and the path is filled with pitfalls. This idea can be intimidating, especially when you embark on a creative path later than others with more formal training, or concurrently with them but on your own. Don't let your circumstances dissuade you, regardless of your current level of attainment. Let awareness of your strengths and weaknesses inspire you by learning from those who are more skilled, and from those who possess different skills. See item #6 on identifying strengths and weaknesses.
- **Permission.** Give yourself permission to make mistakes, to fail, to take chances—and to succeed. Take small chances at first, and then larger ones. Taking chances is like playing poker. You bet small at first, when your holdings are small. As you gather more chips by making small gains, you take bigger, but nonetheless calculated, chances without risking all your assets.

Composer Ronald J. Brown gives himself wide latitude in making "mistakes," and he's benefitted from this attitude. "I have literally hundreds of works from eight measures to complete symphonic movements that are incomplete 'mistakes,'" he says. "It is a rare completed work that emerges from all those false starts, but the end result is usually worth it."

- **Protection.** Protection accompanies permission. Protection is knowing that making "mistakes" in the creative process is actually beneficial—learning from each "mistake" draws you closer to success. Mistakes let you discover more clearly the path to success. Forge ahead in your creative endeavors, knowing that you will make mistakes and take wrong turns. Today's "mistake" leads to tomorrow's success.

- **Patience.** Patience is knowing that quality, success, and growth take time. Do not be discouraged by what seems to be slow progress. When I look back on my music of some 50 years ago, I see that my composing has greatly evolved. I have listened to others' music voraciously, and from what I have heard I adopted the qualities that I thought were best. Since junior high school, I've studied orchestral scores while listening to music. I have been identifying what I deem to be the best composition, orchestration, structural, and stylistic qualities, and slowly, over the years, I've infused them into my work. I'm still doing that. This process takes time—and patience. See item #6.
- **Persistence.** Persistence goes with patience. Determination is more vital than talent, so practicing stick-to-itiveness is a key to progressing and reaching goals. This idea is so important, it's part of this book's epigraph. It's a guiding principle. Review this guiding principle.
- **Presumption.** I approach my work with certain assumptions. I presume I wield the power to let my creativity and productivity blossom. I presume to give myself permission to fail and to succeed. I presume I am protected from letting mistakes prevail. I presume to have the patience required to learn and grow. I presume to succeed and reach my goals.

4   Overcome procrastination.

Overcoming procrastination is especially difficult for me. Sometimes, admittedly, I cannot overcome procrastination and I succumb to waiting hours, days, weeks, or, regrettably, months, to continue a project. It's difficult to know when you need such a break to let an idea or project simmer, or when you're just procrastinating. Most of the time, these seven techniques help me stop stalling:

1 Create a to-do list. Remove items you complete and add new tasks. The point is never to complete the list until you finish a project, but to revise it continually as you work on a task. Be persistent and accomplish those items on the list. Your to-do list gives you direction and focus. It gives you something about which to get excited. It gives you a reason to rush to the computer each day. Keep prioritizing your list so that it guides you through each project. Maintaining to-do lists can also increase productivity.

A to-do list is the smallest division in spelling out goals. See item #19 in the next section, "Set goals and measure progress."

Composer Rain Worthington offers a valuable caveat concerning to-do lists and procrastination: "As a creative artist, it's oh so easy to undermine yourself with practical roadblocks and excuses," she says. "I often remind myself, 'Thinking about something is not the same as doing something!' Being aware of a deadline is not actually submitting works by that deadline. With a to-do list hanging over you, it's hard to clear your mind for your music. So I don't delay in getting things done on my to-do lists. In this way, I don't allow the business things of career to build up as ongoing brain clutter, crowding out the creative space."

2 When I finish a composing session, I often write a small note on what to do next, including both where to start physically in a document and ideas on its content. These notes further prevent procrastination and let me continue a train of creative thought. In Finale, I create text boxes in scores with these kinds of notes.

3 Becoming blocked while working on a piece could be a sign that something is wrong with the music I'm working on. I'm always on the lookout for this kind of impediment. My procrastination in these kinds of situations means that I don't like some aspect of what I wrote but I haven't yet identified exactly what's disagreeable. I know myself and my creative process well enough to realize I need to change the melodic line, give it to a different instrument, change the harmony, rework the instrumentation, add or take away measures in some places, or change the key or time signature, for example. At this point, I will leave the piece untouched for a while because I know the solution will come to me. I might mark the troublesome spot in the music and write notes to myself for my return to the music. I believe these kinds of notes also prompt my subconscious mind to solve the problem while I engage in other activities.

Finnish composer Ari Romppanen has a similar solution to being blocked. "In my case, procrastination sometimes derives from uncertainty about some new idea, or some kind of 'writer's block,' in which I just can't start writing a new piece or section," he says. "In these cases, I usually do something different—read a book, go to an art gallery, or listen to different music, for example. Besides helping to start something new, these activities also help to bring forth new ideas."

In my experience, if you're blocked, you might also try rearranging the layout of your work area. Move your desk to a different side or corner of your office, for instance, and rearrange your other office furniture accordingly. Rearranging an office might be difficult because of one's electrical and wifi needs. Still, examine your workplace and consider if moving things around might help. This idea is similar to my ploy for gaining a fresh perspective when I edit my work—working elsewhere than my office.

4 Divide and conquer. You are reading the result of dividing an enormous, complex project into smaller tasks and accomplishing those tasks one by one—divide and conquer. Writing a book, or a musical work, can be a daunting project—so many parts and tasks!

This book began as a collection of lessons I had learned over the years, and as I added to it, the outline took shape. On 3x5 cards I wrote down all the lessons I had learned. I added lessons on cards as I thought of them, and I ordered them logically. That organizing led to my establishing the two main book sections. As I added to the outline, I began writing a query and a full book proposal. In a similar manner I outlined the book query and full book proposal, beginning with essential information I wanted to include, and then fleshing out each section.

I apply the same strategy when I prepare a musical piece for publication or for performance. I consider the tasks required to prepare the score, the parts, and my performance notes. Then I accomplish each task, beginning with score preparation. For more details on music preparation, see item #17, "Ensure your work's professional appearance," in the next section.

5 Sometimes, procrastinating means that I need to distance myself from a project to let it "simmer." I often stop mulling over my music in these periods, and solutions and direction often come to me this way. How ironic it is that practical solutions often appear when I'm not thinking about them! I've discovered that these periods often follow intervals of much composing. I don't fret over beginning these periods—I know they are part of my creative process. In the same way I conjure up musical ideas—at any time and anywhere, day or night—directions and solutions to problems come, and with my note paper and iPhone handy, I'm ready to write down or record these ideas and problem solutions.

These kinds of problem solutions often come to me as I lay quietly in bed, waiting to fall asleep. No problem—when the "Eureka" moment comes, I turn on the light, grab my iPhone or notepad, and write down the solution.

6 I have observed my creative process long enough to know not only when to take a break but also when to police myself back to the tasks at hand. When a new idea, amplification, change, new direction, or solution appears, I either notate it right away, or begin working on it (if I'm at or near my computer). I don't wait to set down items when they come because I know that if I wait, I will likely lose those ideas.

This skill is surprisingly difficult to master because these kinds of ideas and solutions come not in booming thunderclaps, but more often in quiet, fleeting inklings and sudden, subtle "aha" moments while I'm engaged in unrelated activities. I've worked at cultivating the skill of recognizing these flashes for what they are, and establishing the discipline of harnessing them on notepaper or on my iPhone.

7 Another way to minimize procrastination is to establish routines at the same times every day during which you compose, study, and conduct research and promotion. My practice includes composing in the morning, evening, and late at night; proofreading and editing after dinner; and conducting research and promotion early in the afternoon.

Brazilian composer Divan Gattamorta says, "I've established rules of time for my day-to-day activities—time to study, time to write, time to rest, and so on." A routine like this helps him remain disciplined and leads him back to the tasks at hand if he strays.

Composer Christopher Carlone offers a different take on procrastination. "Procrastination is a huge factor for me and all my freelance media composing friends," he says. "We often take on as many gigs as we can and prioritize the ones we are most excited about (because of content, pay, or artistic direction). I have discovered that my procrastination has improved when I take fewer 'free' and 'exposure' gigs and focus more on gigs that value my time and work. Composing should never be all about the money, but artists can never lie to themselves and say that it doesn't feel good when their art is considered valuable by others."

Composer Laurie Jeanne Crockett has yet another take on procrastination. "I cannot piecemeal a project," she says. "When I finally decide 'it's time' and get around to tackling a project, I dive headlong into it. I set a day or several days aside, depending on the project, and just plow through it. Having an actual deadline and knowing it's approaching is usually what helps me decide 'it's time' and overcome procrastination. If the deadline is up to me, I try very hard to stick to the timeline I've set for myself and not move it just because I can. That part comes down just to discipline."

Composer Ari Romppanen connects just being plain lazy with procrastination. "Sometimes procrastination exists only because of laziness," he says. "Then you just have to kick yourself and just do it. And the best medicine for that is a deadline."

U.S.-based composer Teresa O'Connell agrees. "I actually work best with a deadline," she says, "so I create a deadline if there isn't an actual project completion date imposed by someone else. Once I get started, I truly don't want to stop until the composition is complete."

U.S.-based composer Pamela Illanes-Tatsuoka takes both a philosophical and practical view of overcoming procrastination. "Procrastination has always been an issue for me, but I am able to overcome the problem because I know the importance of finishing what I've started," she says. "Sometimes you want to be perfect, write perfect, feel perfect, but this is not reality. Life is not perfect, and nobody is perfect in this life, so I know my work cannot be perfect, either, but my music is an expression of what I feel and what I want to try to express. Procrastination for me is how I avoid the imperfections of my work and of life, so I must remember to embrace them and these hard moments."

In contrast, composer Grahame Gordon Innes doesn't try to overcome procrastination. "I let my procrastination take its course," he says. "When it's over, my work advances in some new direction."

5 Let experience and practice help you identify your artistic style, musical strengths, and composing preferences.

As you read, listen to, and analyze the music of others, you gradually absorb new insight and understanding that you can apply to your own work. Combinations of a wealth of these insights and applying them in your projects over time—a long time—become your individual "style." Individual style can change this way, too. This accumulation of insights, knowledge, and skills can increase your storehouse of creative solutions to problem areas in your compositions. That is, as your arsenal of skills grows, your technique and stylistic choices increase.

Here are some examples of musical observations that have proven important to me. They reveal the kinds of ideas I've gleaned from other music, and they can show you how to do the same. I've used these musical insights to compose my own music.

- Lennon-McCartney and others' songs. The phrases of their catchiest melodies include an interval of a 4th, 5th, 6th, or greater. In my more advanced works, I try to include such an interval leap or two in my melodic lines. Composer Glenn Martin adds, "Henry Mancini's 'Moon

River' and 'Days of Wine and Roses' also come to mind. These songs, among many others, taught me to write intervallic leaps in my melodies."

- Compose interesting melodic lines, solo or otherwise, for all the instruments. Mozart, Beethoven, Brahms, Hindemith, Leonard Bernstein, and Mahler symphonies are some of my inspiration for composing memorable melodies. When I was an undergraduate student at the Eastman School of Music, students would judge orchestral works by the quality of the musical lines for their instruments and for other instruments. When I compose, I still think this way: I ask myself, "would this be fun to play and hear?"

    Composer Ronald J. Brown thinks similarly. "I always watch the musicians at a concert and imagine what each is doing to contribute to the overall effort," he says. "I sympathize with the violists during a Haydn symphony, endlessly playing the same two or three notes, or the trombonists during a Verdi opera who must sit quietly for 20 or 30 minutes and then play a cadence. I try to write interesting parts for all my musicians."

- Borodin string quartet no. 2. I've loved this piece ever since junior high school. My listening to it and studying the score revealed the balance Borodin achieves in all the parts and the importance of each part. That is, the piece isn't just an accompaniment to the soprano (1st violin) voice. I've applied this insight into all my music, especially my chamber pieces.
- Brahms Fourth Symphony, 1st and 4th movements. I've always been amazed at the variety of tonal colors and

moods Brahms achieves in the 4th movement—a theme and variations. I have also noticed that Brahms had a way of "wrapping things up" to signal a work's coda. I've noticed his heralding the end in the first movement, too.
- Beethoven's 7th Symphony, 2nd movement. What a lesson in orchestration of woodwind groupings and trying new rhythms and harmonies!
- Mozart's "Kyrie" from his "Requiem" is one of the best examples of counterpoint. I never tire of listening to it. In fact, I've been so taken with the "Kyrie" that I arranged it for concert band. That arrangement is published at pdfbandmusic.com.
- Handel's "Messiah" is one example I've noticed of placing voices in their "singable" ranges (goes for instruments, too). This "singability" is evident to me in "For Unto Us a Child Is Born," and the "Amen," just to mention two examples.
- Bock/Harnick "Fiorello!" I love the countermelodies in "The Bum Won." In "The Music Man," I've noted the countermelodies in "Lida Rose" and "Will I Ever Tell You."
- In much music I notice fresh chord variety and melodic hooks. I hear these qualities often in Rodgers & Hammerstein's music, Brahms symphonies, and Humperdinck's "Evening Prayer" from "Hansel and Gretel." Mussorgsky's "Promenade" from "Pictures at an Exhibition" is another good example of captivating chords.
- Dr. Darrell Scott was my music theory teacher for two years at the Eastman School of Music. He used to say that when a composer did something catchy, he repeated it. As we analyzed Bach chorales, for instance, Dr. Scott

would say, "If it sounds nice, do it again!" I've applied this little but effective technique in much of my own music, adding repeats, repeating sections with some variation, or repeating sections, perhaps with variation, later in the music.

Keeping up with this kind of practice pays big dividends. Composer Glenn Martin calls it his "toolbox." "Have a toolbox of techniques that you can use when called upon to write a piece," he says. "Your toolbox should include skills like general harmonic vocabulary that you like, contrapuntal techniques (your way of doing it), and forms and ways of stringing together ideas. Form and the way your ideas and themes flow are very important. Learn to have the right amount of 'continuity and variety' (sameness and differentness) in your composing. This skill is the key to keeping the listener engaged and listening to your music, the mind not drifting away from the music. Beethoven was a master at this, as were Tchaikovsky, Rachmaninoff, and Howard Hanson."

Another maxim I've embraced is that as you grow and experiment, stop trying to be brilliant. Beginning composers often fall into this trap. Trying to compose ground-breaking, genius, or "new" music often leads to amateurish results—mixed styles, incomplete form, hodgepodges of fragments, and inane music.

As I said at the beginning of this item, finding a pleasing balance of freshness and skill in composing takes much time and much practice. It occurs gradually as you gain new insights into your music and into the music of others. It occurs as you learn nuances of composing techniques. It occurs as you become increasingly familiar with many musical forms, styles, and disciplines of music theory. And it occurs with continually evaluating and refining your composing results through your own evaluation and the constructive ideas of others.

For these reasons, regularly seeking feedback on your work helps you smooth your works' rough spots. Over time, the little changes you make to your music and the insights you gain this way give your music maturity and depth. Remember that this is, of course, a long process.

6 Identify your strengths and weaknesses.

I don't think there is a secret to one's identifying strengths and weaknesses as musicians and composers, nor do I believe it's difficult to do so—we know where we shine and where we falter. If you think you're lacking in some areas, identify those weaknesses and work at them. Identify your strengths, too, and devise ways you can capitalize on them. Turning weaknesses into strengths is a slow process that takes time and requires much patience. For me, I understand my strengths and weaknesses better as I continually assess my skills and output.

One way I measure my composing skills is to evaluate my output. For example, I've identified inadequate development of some of the motifs in my music that I wrote years ago. Through hearing fine examples of theme development in others' music and identifying many ways in which composers create smooth development and continuity, I've learned to apply different techniques to my music to create more pleasing sections of development.

One of my biggest regrets as a composer, and what I perceived for a long time as a weakness, is not becoming a more skilled pianist. I had started clarinet lessons in 4th grade, and by 6th grade I was also playing saxophone and flute, and noodling at the piano. In high school I also studied cello so that I could better learn how to compose for strings. I had also been singing in choirs through high school. My parents initiated piano lessons for me, also when I was in high school, but I didn't practice to improve. I understand theory and chords from noodling at the keyboard, and I can identify and hear melodies and chords without a keyboard, but not practicing ensured that my technical facility would not improve. It didn't. I relied on "ear." Ironically, I just didn't understand the process of improving with practice.

I developed a belief that my lack of technical piano skills prevented my taking in different styles and lyric and accompaniment qualities, inherent in piano music. I soon believed that the lack of piano skills limited my skill and growth as a composer.

Now, though, I don't believe this idea, at least not entirely so. I've embraced composing without a piano, so much so that I now doubt my long-held belief that my lack of piano skills was a detriment. Maybe then it was a disadvantage, but now it's not because I've overcome it with the ideas that fill this book.

To conquer this difficulty, I realized that I compose lines first—melodies and motifs—and then I create harmony, or contrapuntal lines in other voices. Identifying this approach helped me embrace it.

This understanding has taught me to accept my cumulative skills and experience. It has let me delve more vigorously into my composing, and it's increased my productivity. Perhaps this path took me in a direction that I somehow needed to follow. It has let me "go with what I got."

"Starting with a base of 'going with what you got' and building on it, we continue amassing knowledge," says Canadian composer Laura Pettigrew. "In pursuit of any career, having the dedication and passion to achieve a goal and committing to the long haul increases the results exponentially. This process creates new synapses as we train our brain, which encodes information. Through this process we can identify our strengths and weaknesses and, most importantly, we can discover how we as unique individuals learn and process information."

The trick, then, after identifying, or at least, becoming aware of, your strengths and weaknesses, is to capitalize on your strengths and improve on your weaknesses.

Composer Michael J. Miller says, "I stick to what I'm good at, and never apologize for being 'me.' That said, I'm not afraid of realizing what others do better than me. When I come across something great done by another composer, I try to imitate and learn the technique, and add it to my creative toolbox."

Composer Laurie Jeanne Crockett has identified her strengths and takes advantage of them. "I have an ear for melody," she says. "I capitalize on this strength by writing sacred vocal pieces and instrumental pieces with strong lyrical lines. Because theory is not my strong suit, I take advantage of YouTube tutorials and keep several music theory books at the ready for reference."

Composer Divan Gattamorta sums up his strategy this way: "I am always aware of what I can do and what I can't do. My motto is, 'Don't do what you don't know'."

Composer Glenn Martin's experience is similar to mine. "Stay within your limit of knowledge, while continually expanding it," he advises. "A favorite Ayn Rand quote I have on my wall: 'Live and act within the limit of your knowledge and keep expanding it to the limit of your life.'"

Some composers endure much introspection to identify their strengths and weaknesses. Consider one aspect of U.S.-based composer Alex Shapiro's journey in this area as she struggled with a career-wide view of identifying strengths and weaknesses and how she clarified them:

"Being an adept composer means being an adept editor who's brutally honest with oneself," she says. "Growing as a composer means exploring many creative avenues and taking some risks, because composers don't always immediately know where their strongest talents lie.

"In my case, after I left my composition studies at the Manhattan School of Music in New York City, I moved to Los Angeles and worked scoring film and TV projects. After 15 years, I reached a point at which I realized that I was no longer happy in that part of the business, but I knew that I still wanted to make my living as a composer.

"One day, I drew up a simple spreadsheet. The rows listed all the many genres of music in which I enjoy composing, and a few music-related job ideas (for example, executive director of an arts advocacy organization). The columns waited for ranked checkmarks, in the form of frank assessments about how competent—or not—I truly believed I was in each genre, and, very importantly, how happy I believed I'd be were I to choose that path.

"In my search for the next phase of my career, I discovered four essential questions to ask myself:
1. What do I love doing/composing?

2. What do I love doing/composing that I'm NOT that great at?
3. What am I really adept at that I would NOT love doing?
4. What do I love doing/composing that I actually believe I'm pretty good at?

'"I made a conscious point to omit money/earning a living from any row or column. I believe that we have the most chance at a happy and successful career when we pursue that which comes naturally to us. The important thing is to determine what that might be!

"One of the last feature films I scored was written for chamber orchestra, with no synths on the date. This was both unusual for a low budget film and very rewarding artistically. The experience had reawakened my love of acoustic chamber music.

"Looking at a spreadsheet that proclaimed my love of writing pop songs, jazz tunes, musical theatre, film music, and concert music, it became clear that of all these choices, the one that tugged at me the strongest, was the latter. I focused all of my energies in that direction, and within a couple of years the result was commissions, performances, and recordings. It was the right choice!"

Shapiro surmises, "So the lesson is to listen to your heart, be aware of what you most love composing, and write the music that you want to hear."

7 Seek feedback and constructive criticism on your work.

Without developing a thick skin, you cannot learn from feedback, so develop the ability to withstand harsh criticism. Consider all criticism carefully, constructive or not.

Composer Ronald J. Brown explains why he values constructive criticism. "The first thing I do when I complete a work is post it to www.composeforums.com for feedback," he says. "Forum membership ranges from beginners to seasoned professionals, but I read each comment carefully and incorporate many suggestions. The trouble with reviewing one's own work is that we tend to see what we think is there, or what we intended, rather than what is actually there. That's the value of seeking constructive criticism."

Composer Pamela Illanes-Tatsuoka thinks similarly. "I think it's very important to accept constructive criticism and feedback," she says. "Not everyone will like your music and they will surely give you criticism. I learn from this kind of critique because it is a new perspective that can help me clarify my own ideas. Sometimes criticism may hurt, but I am grateful for it because it allows me to learn."

Sometimes the medium in which you compose determines why and how you negotiate criticism. "I'm a composer of dance music," says Composer Divan Gattamorta. "This means that I constantly must evaluate and listen to criticism and feedback. I also send my work to other composers for their opinions."

Composer Sahlia Wong seeks ideas from specific people. "I seek out advice from colleagues on all levels. When you expand your network, you can get a sense of which of your contacts have certain strengths and skills that you may still be developing," she says. "I believe these people are our greatest resources for helping to improve our own craft."

In addition, enter juried competitions and contests that offer constructive feedback, but weigh heavily competitions with high entry fees—I generally avoid these contests.

I occasionally face tempo disagreements with conductors, for instance. I have no idea why, but some performances of my works are way too fast. You always want constructive ideas, but even nastiness can be helpful. In a disagreement with a conductor about a tempo, for instance, I try to explore the criticism to understand it fully. That can be difficult when you're gritting your teeth through someone's acerbity, but just keep your goal in mind—understanding the criticism so that you can judge its applicability to your work and make changes you deem appropriate to make the work better.

I give criticizers the benefit of the doubt, so I assume that the criticism in these disagreements is offered from a constructive standpoint, regardless of the tone or language in which it's delivered.

Even when criticism is helpful, getting someone to clarify a comment on a specific musical or artistic element or nuance can be difficult. Patiently questioning criticism this way may seem pointless and patronizing and sometimes self-demeaning. But criticism is often feelings about the music, so it's sometimes difficult to translate "I don't like it," to a more specific, "The tempo is too slow," or "I don't care for the harmonization," or "The clarinets should play this part, not the trumpets." If you can elicit this kind of specific criticism, it's worth trying. I try to be tactful and effective without inflection in my questioning, and I try to keep it brief and focused. Getting critiquers to clarify their thoughts makes criticism the most helpful.

I often post my music works on composeforums.com, and I have occasionally posted works on the Facebook forums Tonal Composers, Actual Tonal Composers, Music Composition Analysis & Feedback, and Composers. The feedback in these forums is always helpful. Seek similar support from fellow composers and teachers.

Composer Teresa O'Connell says, "I am comfortable asking many of my musician friends and colleagues for critiques. My husband and two daughters all have music degrees, and they are also good sources of feedback."

Composer Ari Romppanen offers still another idea on getting constructive criticism. "The best way to seek feedback on your work is to discuss your work with other composers and listen to their music," he says. "But it's surprisingly difficult to have a very detailed conversation with other composers about their works. At the moment I'm involved in a project in which several performing artists (from theater, dance, and circus) gather together and we talk about our own work, go to theater or ballet together and talk about the performances. I've found it very fruitful to talk about construction of compositions with dramatists, for example.

We discussed an article about writing children's plays, and a discussion about it with a professor of directing in the theatre academy was very illustrative and gave me many ideas how to develop my own musical works."

8   Conquer not being good enough.

I often compare my music competitively to that of others in terms of "better" and "worse." I learned such fierce competitive behavior in high school. I auditioned every year for all-county and all-state band, and during three summers as a high school camper at Interlochen's National Music Camp, students competed weekly for ensemble chair assignments. I did well competing. In 1965, as a high school junior, and in 1966 as a senior, I made first chair clarinet in the Central New Jersey Region II band. In 1965 I placed 7th chair in allstate band, and in 1966 I placed 2nd chair in allstate band. However, I dropped out of allstate band my senior year because of a conflict with a show pit orchestra to which I had a commitment.

I remind myself often that all composers have strengths and weaknesses. I am free to work on weaknesses, if I want. I capitalize on what I've identified as my strengths, and I steer those assets toward my music publication goals. I learn from others' music, identifying elements I like and parts I dislike, and I incorporate into my own music a mixture of all the elements that appeal to me. I believe that's how creativity and composing work.

I need to remind myself that a "better or worse" comparison is inappropriate. I remind myself often to change "better" and "worse" to "different." When I compare my music to that of others, I learn much more from a "how is this different" perspective than I learn from a "how is this better or worse" standpoint.

The kind of competitiveness that I came to embrace stifled my creativity and gutted my productivity. Examine your attitude in this respect and overcome this bane, as I did.

Composer Rain Worthington offers a valuable perspective on competing. "Creativity is not a competition and art is not a competitive pursuit," she says. "I need to remind myself of these ideas as I receive notices that my works were not among the score call selections or prizes awarded. Similarly, this idea is good to keep in mind when pieces are chosen, or when they do receive recognition. A genuine generosity and expansiveness of spirit is essential for staying positive and productive. The recognition and successes of any individual composer promote awareness of contemporary classical music and benefit all composers working in the field."

9 Tame your internal editing, critical mind.

Our internal creative naysayer is always on, always detracting us, and always ruthlessly critiquing—and sometimes stifling—our output. Our internal naysayer is the king of procrastination and doubt. That's why this task is one of the most difficult among creative people, but it's one of the most valuable skills for increasing productivity and tapping one's talent.

I often need to turn the naysayer off because I'm my own worst critic! I use certain techniques to turn my internal critic off. These ideas are one way I grant myself permission to experiment and grow—vital to any creative effort. Cultivating these skills and knowing when to apply them take practice. When my composing flows, I don't need to wield these tools. But sometimes when my composing slows and I reach an impasse, I use the following techniques.

First, I select a few measures of music, a phrase, say, eight or 16 measures. This music can be something from a piece I'm currently composing or a snippet of work I've completed. Then I allow myself to edit, change, rewrite, or reorchestrate that section completely without debilitating internal criticism or adverse consequence—no matter the outcome.

Second, I often play a game in which I step out of myself and become a different composer, someone completely free of the critical chains in which I felt bound. I then work on the piece, constantly reminding myself that I'm now [a great composer who I admire].

The results of these techniques often surprise me with something better than my original, or new ideas that fuel new projects. With these approaches, I've also come up with musical solutions to problems that have blocked my progress on a piece. Sometimes the results aren't appropriate or otherwise don't work, but that's OK. I keep trying.

Here's another strategy: "I turn off my internal critic by doing activities outside of my artistic world, such as cooking and visiting friends and my parents," says Composer Divan Gattamorta. "In addition, I've broken up my composing time by taking walks and exercising."

Canadian composer Sahlia Wong uses a different strategy to tame her internal critic. "I have been practicing meditation to overcome the internal critical voice," she says. "This may seem counter-intuitive or even counter-productive, but I believe that the more you practice turning off the self-critical voice in one sector, the easier it will be to apply it to other areas, such as when you actually sit down to compose. In addition, I am guilty of being self-critical to the point at which I don't even start to write a note. But it's a different story when I'm working on a professional project with a deadline. The internal critical voice may still be there, but I'm more forced to ignore it because it's important to have the project finished in a timely manner."

Other composers view their internal naysayers differently. "I don't turn the internal critic off, partly because it is what makes me a better creator," say composer Christopher Carlone. "Even greats like Sonny Rollins were known for never being satisfied with their own musicianship. That said, you must strike a balance between criticism and contentment. I think it is OK to be proud of your work, but never satisfied. So the internal naysayer stays on."

U.S.-based composer Kim Diehnelt thinks similarly. "I'm constantly reviewing my work with a critical ear and eye," she says. "Sometimes I can tell a passage or measure lacks conviction, but I don't (yet) know why. I'm comfortable moving on and returning to those spots later. Also, while composing, I'm deep in focus, listening—deep listening. When I'm in this type of thought, there is no space for the ego to add comments."

Composer Pamela Illanes-Tatsuoka says that her internal critic is always there, "but over the years I've learned that my best compositions are the ones that come naturally and flow to me without interference. So I've learned to suppress self-criticism as I create. If you are lucky, you are able to compose in that moment without thought. If you get into critical mode, you begin to destroy the beauty of such a spontaneous creation. This is why I try to avoid such negative thoughts. The one note or four notes that you may change as a result of such negativity may destroy the piece. As a composer, I very much respect and appreciate these spontaneous moments—they are a gift from God."

Composer Ari Romppanen strikes a balance with his internal critic. "I think it's important to maintain some criticism on what you are doing," he says. "For me, the question is how not to give internal criticism too much power. Without criticism you can easily resort to easy solutions, and you keep repeating yourself, so a certain amount of criticism helps you develop your own work and makes you strive for better and better solutions."

In a similar light, composer Teresa O'Connell harnesses the internal critic. "I think turning off my internal critic is nearly impossible," she says. "But I am fortunate to have a musician best friend who loves for me to try out my music and ideas on her in the very early stages. The validation of someone I trust helps me press on, in spite of intense self-doubt."

Canadian composer Elizabeth Raum tames her internal critic with a "filter." "I never turn off my internal critic," she says. "I have a good 'taste filter' and a bad memory so when I write something, I can come back to it the next day and listen to it as if for the first time and know whether it's good or needs work."

Finnish composer Jukka Viitasaari also works with his internal critic. "I try to be patient and let the composition I'm working on hatch a little," he says. "I'm good with deadlines, so working with a deadline helps me tame my internal critic."

U.S.-based composer Mark Taylor has a different viewpoint: "I think I might not be critical enough," he says. "I tend to compose something and keep moving. I rarely go back and revise or edit unless it's a project for someone else (like a film score), where I get notes that need to be addressed. I'm sure much of my work could benefit from some additional scrutiny and polishing. I think it's important to be able to shift gears from 'creative guy' to 'critical guy,' though. When you're in the groove and the music is flowing, just try to get it all down and have fun creating. Then it'll be time to look at the work more objectively and see what can be done to make it better."

10 Recognize a mentor if one appears, and tap your mentor's knowledge and skills.

There are subtle but vital differences between a teacher and a mentor. A teacher passes on skills and technique. A mentor provides perspective and guidance through advice in addition to passing on skills and technique. Having a mentor is like having a personal guidance counselor. Mentors are so valuable! Always be on the lookout for a mentor.

One of my first mentors was Everett Gates, head of the music education department at the Eastman School of Music in the late 1960s. Mr. Gates encouraged me and supported me when I thought others did not—and when I didn't believe in myself! Always encouraging and positive, he inspired me to delve deeply into my studies, and to expand my studies into areas about which I was unaware. We stayed in touch for several years after I graduated, and in his honor, my wife and I named our son after him, so great was his influence on me personally and professionally.

Another mentor was Lou Bynum, my first boss in my first teaching job and head of the music department in then Liberty (NY) Junior-Senior High School. Lou was always supportive and instructive. He was a terrific supervisor, manager, and friend. I learned so much from Lou about teaching and working with colleagues and parents!

Composer Laura Pettigrew speaks of the value of having a mentor. "A mentor is a valuable guide in identifying strengths and weaknesses because a mentor has already undergone the developmental stages of honing one's craft," she says. "Thus, a mentor can provide the most useful feedback and guidance."

Pettigrew says, "Following my education in nursing, I returned to university at age 37 to pursue a degree in performance, and during a composition class with Dr. Thomas Schudel, he fortuitously said, 'Laura, you're a composer.' Subsequently, my career path changed to composition, having my first work published as an undergraduate by Alry Publications. After I completed my bachelor of music degree, I pursued a masters degree in composition with Dr. Schudel. I am forever grateful for his mentorship."

Composer Rain Worthington also speaks of the value of having mentors. "I have been fortunate to have several important people who have helped me at different stages in my career," she says. "As an early mentor, composer Charlemagne Palestine generously offered the use of his loft space and beautiful Bosendorfer piano for my first solo piano concerts. In forming my new music ensembles, Zone and Hizohi, I worked with some terrific musicians who stuck with me through all the rehearsals and very, very late-night gigs at some seemingly improbable performing spaces on the downtown New York City music scene. And when I started to compose for orchestra and began to pursue recordings of my works as a way to document my orchestral music, a longtime dear friend offered support for the recording sessions with PARMA Recordings. At each of these stages, these mentors were career changers for which I am forever grateful."

"Most of my mentors came to me as a result of my professional activities as a hornist on the New York City 'avant' jazz scene," says Composer Mark Taylor. "Since there aren't many hornists in jazz, anyway, on the rare occasion that someone needed one it was a pretty short list before they got to me. Consequently, I spent a lot of time surrounded by older, very accomplished musicians/bandleaders/improvisers who provided a wealth of information—sometimes by my just sitting there and listening to them talk about 'the good old days.' My main composition mentors (after grad school) were Henry Threadgill and Muhal Richard Abrams, who strongly encouraged me to listen, listen, listen to lots of music (and lots of different kinds of music). They treated me as though the worth and value of anything I might produce was a foregone conclusion, and they pushed me to experiment and figure out what it was that I wanted to express through my writing, playing, and bandleading."

Find a mentor

I found my mentors through serendipity, but you can acquire a mentor, or mentors, on purpose. To find a mentor, identify the area in which you would like mentorship—an aspect of composing, how to market your work to publishers, gaining more performances, or becoming more proficient on an instrument, for example. Then create a list of experts in these fields who could be your "candidate" mentors. A direct approach, as in, "Hey, wanna be my mentor?", is inappropriate. Your mentor should benefit from the relationship, too, so think of ways in which you could assist your mentor. Internships and apprenticeships are one avenue. See item #12 in the second section, "Engage in an internship or apprenticeship," for more information on internships.

In addition, you could identify someone in your specialty who you think might mentor you. Then email this person a question. Base your question on information you don't know that you could use in your composing. If you get a useful answer, apply the information in your work, and then let your proposed mentor know that you were able to apply the information in your composing. This kind of exchange can lead to your asking more questions, receiving helpful, applicable answers, and engaging in beneficial exchanges. Such professional interaction could lead to face-to-face meetings, collaboration, and mentorship. Be patient in this process.

Some Facebook newsgroups offer a "Find a Mentor" option, in which you can "share your experience or learn valuable skills from someone in your group." The option is available in "select groups focused on parenting, professional and personal development." When you bring up a newsgroup with the mentoring option, an announcement about it may appear. If you're uncertain which groups include this option, contact the group's administrator.

LinkedIn has a similar option called "Career Advice." To reach "Career Advice," navigate to your profile and look for it beneath your title, headline, and description.

With both the Facebook and LinkedIn options, you can also become a mentor.

11 Take courses locally and online.

Music notation and DAW (digital audio workstation) software can be complicated, so until you become proficient in using it, that software remains more of a liability in your work than an asset. For this reason, you might consider DAW and notation software courses; sound library courses on use and integration with notation and production software; and ear-training, music theory, and orchestration courses. Websites for programs you use likely have tutorials and a wealth of how-to materials and videos. Search YouTube for instructional videos and tutorials periodically because updated and new tutorials appear regularly. Consider anything and everything to enrich your understanding of your art and build your skills with its tools. Tutorials and courses can be especially valuable in light of your identifying weaknesses. Join product support forums, and participate regularly. On these forums you'll often find links to training materials and videos. See the Resources section for more online resource suggestions.

12 Experiment with musical, stylistic, and orchestration techniques.

Step out of your creative safe zone, have some fun, take a chance, and try different techniques, instrument combinations, and musical styles.

I experimented a few years ago by composing a piece that features a band's euphonium, trombone, and baritone players. I envisioned composing a piece with all of these players standing in front of the band. I visualized the audience's excitement and anticipation as all the trombone, euphonium, and baritone players lined up in front of the band. I wanted the piece to be upbeat and exciting, so that the audience would be clapping with the music and want an encore. Thus, I composed "Euphotrombotonia" (yoo-fō-trom-bō-tōn-ee-uh). I derived the name, of course, from a combination of the words "euphonium," "trombone," and "baritone." In 2014, "Euphotrombotonia" was named a winner in the 3rd Annual Sul Ross State University (Texas, USA) Wind Ensemble Composition Contest—all because I gave myself permission to experiment. "Euphotrombotonia" is published by Bell Music Publishing.

When I was about five or six, I remember my parents taking dancing lessons with their friends. I recall the cha-cha tune to which they practiced and learned this dance (such was the 1950s). To this day, every cha-cha I hear reminds me of that time, and I always associated good feelings and carefree fun with that music. So a few years ago, I decided to experiment a bit, and I came up with a Grade 2 concert band piece, "Bluesy Chalumeau Cha-Cha." This piece is published by Alry Publications.

Another experimental piece involved string orchestra and percussion. I've been composing for string orchestra for many years, so that wasn't new. But writing a piece for string orchestra and percussion was new territory for me. The trick, I presumed, was to let the strings and percussion blend without one overpowering the other. I came up with "Terpsichore's Dance," for string orchestra and optional percussion (one player—snare drum, tambourine, and triangle). "Terpsichore's Dance" appears as the third movement in "Dance Suite," published by Gusthold Music Publisher.

Another experiment: I'd never composed anything before for brass quintet, so composing for this ensemble challenged and intrigued me. As I began the piece, I became thoroughly enamored with the traditional brass quintet (two trumpets, F horn, trombone, and tuba)—the sound, the possibilities, and the relative ease with which I could create a score and parts, considering that I had been working with large concert band scores! After an exhilarating few months, I came up with "Brassy Capriccio," for brass quintet. I was so taken with this ensemble that I followed this piece quickly with another brass quintet, "Two Trillion Triplets." Both pieces are published by musicforbrass.com. I've since composed two more brass quintets. Now I'm interested in exploring brass choir and brass band instrumentation—I haven't yet written for brass band. I may dive into that pool soon.

Experimentation pays. You'll learn a lot, gain new insights, expand your horizons, and have fun. Try it! And be sure to seek constructive feedback on your work!

13 Organize your work and stay organized.

Save and back up all your work and idea files—even what you deem to be fragments, mistakes, and wrong turns. Create and maintain a file system that lets you identify previous versions of your work. I use numbers after the titles in file names, such as piece1, piece2, and so forth. For instance, when I was working on a string orchestra piece, the development section of the main motif was giving me trouble—I didn't like any of the directions in which I took the piece. So with each new try, I saved each previous version as title2, title3, title4, and so forth. In this way, I could always develop or amend those previous versions, or perhaps even combine them with a newer version. When I have completed a work and I'm in the final version, I sometimes place the word "final" into the file name right before the extension. I also track a piece's progression and version by its file date, which I also insert before the extension.

Be sure to set up your music notation program so that it backs up your work. This step is important because it saves your work at the source. In Finale, find these settings in Preferences > Save. I specify autosave for 5 minutes and I check "make backups when saving files." I've also created separate directories on my hard drive for these backups and autosaved files. In Finale, both Windows and Mac versions, create the directories on the hard drive and then in Finale specify their location in Preferences > Folders.

U.S.-based composer Raymond Burkhart's organization of materials is similar to mine. "I compose mostly at my computer now, going right from thought to digital 'paper,'" he says. "So all my project ideas are organized in a careful folder and file naming system. I have a folder for my compositions and one for my arrangements of music by others. I give a new work a title, even if just a working title, put the new file in a new folder with the same title, then append to the filename '01.' In time, as I add more music and make changes, I get to a point where I change the file name by changing '01' to '02.' This is essential for keeping track of old versions, which are sometimes handy to look back on, and keeping my work orderly. The latest version always has the highest number at the end of the filename, and not once have I gotten even close to 99 versions!"

Composer Michael J. Miller is meticulous in his organizing his work. "Organization is crucial to success," he says. "The organization scheme doesn't have to be cookie cutter, but you need a system. My files are all catalogued by genre and listed alphabetically. Once a project is finished, I upload it to the cloud, and store it on an external drive in case I ever need to access it again."

Composer Mark Taylor says, "I'm kind of a nerd when it comes to organizing my files and naming conventions. There's a folder for the application (where ALL the Sibelius files go, for example), then another for the year, then one for the project, and then one where I keep old versions after I make revisions, and another for the individual parts once extracted."

I also back up all my work to an external hard drive (a Western Digital 2 TB My Passport), to a networked laptop (a MacBook Air), and in the cloud. Cloud backup is vital in the highly unlikely event that I lose both of my computers and the external drive at the same time. Consider cloud storage. I use iDrive, but choose the company that best meets your needs and whose interface you're most comfortable using. Get recommendations. Several of the most popular and highly rated cloud storage solutions include Backblaze, iDrive, Microsoft OneDrive, Google Drive, Box, Amazon Drive, and Dropbox. There are many others.

Composer Teresa O'Connell says she uses her MacBook Air for everything with Finale. "I write with a digital mini-grand and input manually into Finale," she says. "I store originals in Finale and export PDFs to iCloud and Dropbox. I also have a separate hard drive for storage to be safe, and I email files to myself and have an external hard drive for storage."

Composer Mike Hall says, "Being organized saves time. I frequently work on more than one film as well as two or three album projects, so it's very important to know where everything is. Each project has its own external drive. There are many brands available. After much research, I have found that the Glyph Studio S4000 4TB external hard drive is a good choice."

14 Keep track of your contacts.

What is the best way to keep track of contacts, submissions, performances, and appearances? "This is a good question—as some of the most basic things can turn into stumbling blocks for getting your works out into the world," says composer Rain Worthington. "There is nothing high tech about the way I keep track of submissions, call-for-scores deadlines, performances, etc. For years, I tried to figure out how best to keep track of calls for scores so that I would not miss deadlines. For a while I kept a binder with monthly dividers to keep score calls organized, but I did not check the binder often enough. Now I have the calls in front of me for reference on my desk. I print the score calls, write deadline dates on the pages, and simply have a pile of call information sheets on one side of my desk that I check periodically for approaching deadlines. I find the simplest method works best for me. Similarly, for my own records, I simply track submissions in a document, moving information between headings as I receive word of 'Acceptances,' 'Performances,' and 'Recordings,' or 'Returns/No response.'"

To keep current on who's performing my music and who has promised to send me recordings, I've created and maintain two logs. First, I created a free-form contact log in Microsoft OneNote that lists the piece with the dates and results of my contacts. I now work in Mac OS X, so I transferred that log to the Notes app. Second, to keep track of my submissions for publication, I maintain a log in Microsoft Excel. Before I had created these logs, I kept track of contacts by reviewing my email inbox and relying on my memory. You can imagine what happened. I forgot some promises to send scores and parts, and I missed a few deadlines. My contact logs solved this problem.

You might want to keep track of contacts and activity more formally with contact management software, but so far, I've been doing well with my Notes app and Excel logs.

"Also important is the question of when and what to send out," says composer Rain Worthington. "I figure I now average 40-50 submissions a year. I have learned that for me, it's best to have submissions of my music out in the world for consideration most of the time. No matter the final outcome, it's a way to get your name into the stream of recognition as an 'active' composer, and to be able to introduce some of your work to performing musicians, festivals, presenting organizations, or an orchestra music director. Plus, rejections will be a bit mitigated because there is always a possible acceptance of a work still out there on the horizon. Nevertheless, so many submissions require meticulous tracking."

"I keep submissions in my Dropbox folder so that I can access them from wherever (for instance, if I need to print a score or my CV)," says composer Mark Taylor. "I keep performance and appearance dates in Google Calendar. I keep contacts in Gmail for now. I have been playing around with ZenDesk+Evernote and/or Hubspot, though, so that might be changing. The Google stuff shows up on all my devices and that makes it easy to keep track of what I'm supposed to be doing and when. So far, my life isn't so complicated that I've needed anything more."

Composer R. Duane Hendricks says, "I keep my records in a relatively old computer in my studio. They are not very extensive, just copies of letters and contracts for commissions, copies of scores and parts, and financial entries in a ledger. I'm not very good about keeping copies of programs. Dates of performances appear in my calendar."

Composer Elizabeth Raum doesn't use apps. "I ask for performance programs to be sent to me, either as PDFs or as hard copies, and I save them in yearly folders," she says. "I print out the PDFs so I have everything in hard copy. I am not able to keep track of performances, however, because I often don't know if my works are being performed. I'm a member of SOCAN [Society of Composers, Authors and Music Publishers of Canada], so I get the information for royalties, which reflects performances, but that isn't always possible. Sometimes I find out when a work is performed because it appears on Youtube, or I get an email (or it appears on Facebook)."

Composer Jukka Viitasaari uses no specific app, but he is active in many places online. He says, "I stay up to date often on Facebook, LinkedIn, and the WASBE [World Association for Symphonic Bands and Ensembles] website."

Composer Teresa O'Connell keeps things simple. "I use my iPhone 7 Plus calendar and the Notes app on my iPhone for everything," she says.

Composer Pamela Illanes-Tatsuoka also keeps things simple. "I make sure not to accept so much work at any one time," she says, "so that I can concentrate on the quality of a single project."

Becoming More Educated and Skilled With or Without Formal Music Composition Training

This section includes what I deem to be essential parts of formal and informal learning to compose, and how to make choices in these areas and take advantage of opportunities. Remember that many of the points in the previous section apply concurrently with the points in this section.

1 Be Patient and Persistent.

Learning and growing are lifelong pursuits. This book's epigraph is a steering star for this idea and all the book's ideas, and it is worth repeating here:

> *Nothing in the world can take the place of persistence. Talent will not; nothing is more common than unsuccessful men of talent. Genius will not; the world is full of educated derelicts. Persistence and determination alone are omnipotent.*
> *– Calvin Coolidge, 30th President of the United States*

A sign with this quote hangs on my office wall as a constant inspirational reminder. I am committed to my work and never to give up composing, publishing my music, and learning more about this craft every day.

2   Start and stay mainly with what is most familiar.

This item is the practical application of item #6, "Identify your strengths and weaknesses," in the first section. Without formal assessment and guidance ("placement"), the only way to "know what you need to know" is to set a course based on what you already know.

I started and stayed with education-based concert band, choral, and instrumental ensemble music because these areas encompass the bulk of my training and experience.

If you're just beginning to compose, consider starting by composing music for your main instrument, for ensembles with which you're most familiar, and in genres with which you're comfortable.

I began taking clarinet lessons in fourth grade, and by fifth grade I was noodling on the piano and playing alto saxophone, tenor saxophone, flute, and guitar. I began composing flute and clarinet duets and trios in seventh grade. I became more familiar with other instruments while playing in school bands and pop groups. From elementary school through graduate school, I was in or I directed concert bands, and then I taught instrumental music and was a band director. I've also sung in choruses since junior high school. So my composing focuses on concert bands, instrumental ensembles, and choruses. These areas are my composing comfort zone. I've written for other groups of instruments, but most of my compositions are for concert band, instrumental ensembles, and choruses.

In addition to what's most familiar, compose music about which you are passionate. For instance, for practically my whole life I've been familiar with the prayer, "May the words of my mouth and the meditations of my heart be acceptable to thee, O Lord, my rock and my redeemer" (Psalm 19:14). So I recently created an SATB setting with piano accompaniment. I've also enjoyed Swing-era music, so for concert band I composed "Escapade in Swing," which is published by Imagine Music Publishers, and "Jazzy Capriccio," published by TRN Music Publishers.

Thus, my composing focuses on instruments and genres with which I'm most familiar.

Composer R. Duane Hendricks says, "My musical strengths, or interests, are very important in the types of musical groups for which I compose. My background is very strong in wind ensemble and brass ensemble, so I like to compose most of my works for those groups.

Composer Teresa O'Connell's strategy is similar. "I have lots of experience as a choral director, drama director, and musical director for musical theatre," she says. "I also have vast experience with show choirs as a director and judge, so I lean toward musical theatre and uptempo pop, jazz, rock, and bluesy styles when I compose for K-8. I also love cabaret style, so I write solo works in that style. I also write comedic cabaret."

Composer Raymond Burkhart says, "I think understanding the 'instruments' for which you write is essential, be they the vocal instrument or things played by bands and orchestras, and almost all composers, if they write enough and don't overly restrict themselves, will someday write for an instrument they don't know well," he says. "For me, as a trumpeter and as one who can play all the main brass instruments at least a little, writing for brass has always been a strength, and having also played and studied piano, guitar, string bass, and almost all of the recorders, I've gained valuable insights into writing for piano and organ, some aspects of strings, and to some extent, woodwinds.

"To be a good composer, it's a great help to know not just the basic stuff, like instrument ranges and technical bits, but to know the nuances of qualities of sound in various ranges, how sounds blend, and similar things that typically come only with lots of experience hearing very intelligently a variety of styles and forces. So I always recommend as much listening as possible, writing as much as you can, and getting your work played every chance you get—even if the work isn't finished and even if the musicians aren't the best. One probably learns more by getting played by lesser musicians than by great ones."

3 Learn music theory.

You don't absolutely have to learn anything about music theory to succeed. However, learning music theory—that is, learning music's rudiments—can give you insights into music, your own included, that you might otherwise miss. Furthermore, with a firm basis in music's rudiments, you can better understand other music forms and styles as you progress in your learning.

Composer Elizabeth Raum thinks learning music theory is essential. "I think that's one of the most valuable things you can learn if you want to compose," she says. "Nadia Boulanger apparently felt composition could not be taught, but she did believe in teaching music theory. Many times I've gotten out of a transition fix through basic theory rules. I've also been able to modulate smoothly to a more friendly key for the performer, thanks to my theory background."

Composer Jukka Viitasaari observes, "Years ago, I attended every rock and jazz theory course available. Learning music theory is important because you need to know enough theory not to be bound by it."

Composer Sahlia Wong says, "I believe composers are first and foremost musicians of some sort, and that it is important for us always to keep learning. Knowing something about music theory is part of being a well-rounded musician, so it's important to learn music theory because you don't want to limit yourself by not knowing it. You want to add as many tools as you can to your arsenal. To me, purposely ignoring the chance to acquire more knowledge is unwise."

Composer Raymond Burkhart takes a historical view on the importance of learning music theory. "Sometime during, or just before, the earliest years of my life, all of the traditional constructs of music were either demolished or liberated, depending on your point of view," he says. "Notation was deconstructed accordingly in certain quarters, so learning 'music theory' is only as important as what you need for your kind of composition. We reached 'anything goes' decades ago. But extremes bring responses, and we might owe the resurgence of tonal expression in the 1980s to the minimalists, who re-introduced the C major chord into "new" music, even if you did have to hear it 100 times in succession. Since then, the appeal of, and demand for, music of the extremes has had to make space once again for the composition of music for which there are more traditional tonal and rhythmic structures. This means that whatever kind of music you write, there's probably something about its structure that needs to be learned and mastered. I have benefitted from studying a wide range of theories of music, even if I have not employed them—yet."

From a broader perspective, if "music theory" includes all the elements in various styles and genres of music in which you compose, then learning that "music theory" so that you can apply it in your composing lets you produce material that's structurally and harmonically consistent and that sounds "right." Ironically, learning "music theory" in this light also gives you the freedom to break rules and cross the lines of styles and genres sensibly and tastefully.

4 Consider the music composition curricula of colleges.

I conducted an internet search for "music college course catalog" and came up with a wealth of course listings of the skills that several college music composition programs deem essential. These listings can help guide you because they often reveal subjects and a progression of learning that experienced composers and composition teachers consider to be appropriate. The course listings might suggest topics you may want to pursue, and they could help fill in areas in which you're weak.

5 Study music history.

Music styles and genres are vast and varied, so it pays to study the history of genres and styles that interest you. "If you want to work in the games industry as a composer, learn the history of game music," says composer Zander Hulme. "Music styles in games have arisen from a boiling pot of influences and constraints, and understanding how we arrived where we are now is important and useful learning. In any creative field it will serve you well to know what has and hasn't been done, what the conventions are to follow, which conventions to break, and which rules to bend."

6 Study – and play – the instruments and styles for which you want to compose.

I learned to play other instruments mostly as preparation in a music education degree program to teach those instruments. I also learned much by actually teaching the instruments. I also received cello lessons in high school so that I could become more familiar with writing for strings, and I sang in choirs, which aided—and inspired—my composing choral music.

When I first began getting published in the 1970s, I bought a trumpet and borrowed other instruments to record my music. In a friend's recording studio I dubbed tracks on top of one another. These tapes included my playing flute, clarinet, alto saxophone, tenor saxophone, trumpet, euphonium, and some percussion instruments. I submitted these tapes with scores for publication consideration.

This background, immersion mainly in playing and teaching wind instruments, lets me compose readily and comfortably for these instruments.

7 Play in (or conduct) a community, college, or high school band or orchestra; sing in (or conduct) a community or church choir; or create your own ensemble.

Playing in or conducting an ensemble can help you see not only how instruments fit in to different ensemble settings, but you can also see how players react to the music, suggesting how easy or difficult the music is. Over a longer period, you will also garner an overview of the literature for a particular ensemble, and what is popular in performances both for audiences and players. You would apply these insights into your composing.

Of course, you may be long out of high school or college. Still, you may be able to play in high school and college groups with permission of the ensemble director and school officials.

8 Offer instruction on your primary instrument.

Teaching can have a clarifying effect for you as a musician by your gaining greater insight into the lessons and techniques you pass on to others. Extra income couldn't hurt, either, or you could donate your time.

Composer Glenn Martin also thinks teaching strengthens one's composing. "I teach private lessons on all instruments except oboe and bassoon," he says. "Teaching is a great aid in composing because it puts me one on one with the everyday playing problems of students of all ages and skill levels. Understanding these problems needs to be a part of one's composing technique. That lets you take into consideration the ability level of the player or group for which you are writing."

Contact nearby school instrumental music teachers and ask if they maintain a list of area private teachers. If they do have such a list, ask to be included, and seek their recommending your services to students and parents. Even if they have no such lists, ask ensemble directors to make known your availability to teach private lessons to their school's music booster group. You could also ask to provide a brief introduction to and outline of your teaching strategy and qualifications to school music booster groups in your area.

9 Volunteer your services in your community.

Volunteering is networking: You garner experience this way, add to your resume, meet new people, and promote your name and work. You could offer to entertain at a local hospital, nursing home, or assisted living facility. Similarly, you could create a short lecture for these institutions on an aspect of music with which you're especially familiar.

Consider these other volunteer opportunities:

- Volunteer your services at your church or at other local churches, especially if you play piano or guitar.
- Contact local reputable volunteer organizations that can use volunteer musicians.
- Individual musicians and small ensembles can volunteer to perform at free concerts sponsored by communities and local business organizations.
- Volunteer to teach music appreciation in schools and community centers.
- Volunteer to be an usher at local concert halls and similar venues. In this way, you can listen to performances for free!

- "Volunteer with arts advocacy organizations, both local and national," adds composer Alex Shapiro. "Join committees, organize events, and get to know and support your peers," she says.

10 Become more familiar with music's unfamiliar aspects.

As you experiment with new techniques, specific questions may arise on the new items you discover (see item 12, "Experiment with musical, stylistic, and orchestration techniques," in the previous section). Ask players of instruments that you don't play to demonstrate the instruments' quirks and characteristics: For instance, the awkward "break" for young clarinetists; the trumpet's sharp-sounding "D" and "C#" for beginning trumpet players; the alto, tenor, and baritone saxophone's flat and raspy open fourth-line C#; and for beginning string players, long tones on open E and A strings—players can't use vibrato and the sound is often piercing and unpleasant.

11 Get a private teacher, locally for one-on-one learning, or online.

Many musicians and composers took lessons even while they achieved some success. For instance, after he was commissioned to compose the Concerto in F, a 20-something George Gershwin studied orchestration with prominent American teacher Rubin Goldmark. Gershwin wanted to orchestrate the Concerto in F himself.

Composer Ronald J. Brown is a fan of online learning. "I am almost continuously taking online courses," he says. "Www.Coursera.org is a good resource for university courses, including music, from universities around the world. Other teachers, like Thomas Goss in New Zealand and Alan Belkin in Montreal, have made extensive courses available online, as have many others."

Video calling makes working with a teacher anywhere easy. Skype, FaceTime, GoTo Meeting, Zoom, UberConference, and Google Hangouts are just a few of the possibilities for easy collaboration. See the "Resources" section for website addresses.

Finding a teacher is one thing. Finding the right teacher is another. You should admire, or at least respect, the music of your teacher. Is the teacher's style agreeable, and does it include qualities you'd like to incorporate into your own music? Ask the teacher's students about the teacher's style, temperament, availability and demeanor, and match what you hear with your learning style. Matching your style and goals with a prospective teacher's style and methods helps you the most in the shortest amount of time. Find a teacher who inspires you. Lastly, consider cost.

Composer Sahlia Wong offers useful advice on finding a teacher. "Make sure you try to choose your teachers according to what you specifically want to learn," she says. "I wouldn't just settle for whichever composition teacher or composer is most convenient to see. I'd strive to get time, whether face-to-face or online, with a specific teacher who you think will work best for you when you compare your goals with what a prospective teacher offers. You will also want to do research online and even on social networking sites like Facebook. You can join composer groups from all over the world, in any sector of composing (i.e. concert music, contemporary music, pop, songwriting, film music, etc.), and some of them may offer mentorship programs with various requirements for applying. Get recommendations."

12 Engage in an internship or apprenticeship.

Becoming an intern or apprentice, free or paid, is a great way to create opportunities, find a mentor, meet industry people, hone your skills, and learn new abilities. Consider interning for an experienced teacher, composer, conductor, arranger, copyist, music publisher, record company, music production facility, or ensemble. See item 10 in the previous section on finding a mentor.

13 Listen to and analyze a lot of music—especially the kind of material you want to create.

Spark and fuel your creativity by immersing yourself in music. Just listening to music with no set goal other than enjoyment is valuable. Even just listening for enjoyment, the processes in me of analysis, evaluation, and learning continue. For instance, I'll hear a particularly catchy chord progression, a vibrant rhythmic pattern, an interesting orchestration technique, an especially soaring melody, or a musical style with which I'm unfamiliar. I'll remember where I heard it, and I'll then read it in the score or sheet music. I may not apply their effects for some time, but I know that sooner or later I will apply the techniques and skills I hear in my own way in my own music.

At one time, my score library included some 350 miniature and full-size orchestra and ensemble scores. I would refer to my score library repeatedly. The IMSLP Petrucci Music Library (https://imslp.org) is a good source of now-public domain scores. See the "Resources" section for other similar online resources. This method—casual listening and noting a work's form, harmony, style, melodies, rhythms, instrumentation, and historical context—make up the bulk of my method of music analysis.

Furthermore, listening to a lot of music, all kinds of music, this way, stimulates my creativity. I usually begin hearing a rhythmic pattern or a melody that I repeat in my mind. I may embellish it immediately. Then I write it down or sing it into my iPhone voice memos feature for treatment later. My conjuring ideas is equally immediate or hours and days later—I never know exactly when I'll think up material. Nevertheless, my frequent listening to music often sows the seeds of musical ideas that grow. This process occurs concurrently with the practice that occurs in item #5 in the previous section.

The internet and YouTube are tremendous resources for listening to all kinds of music. Composer Ronald J. Brown puts it this way: "One of the greatest benefits of the Internet is the ability to listen to any music from anywhere in the world at any time. If I had to purchase a record album to hear something new, chances are good I never would have discovered a lot of the gems out there."

Composer Glenn Martin suggests another resource. "Look at Classical Archives-Midi (http://www.classicalarchives.com/midi.html)," he says. "The site includes mostly condensed scores (sometimes full scores) of works by the great masters. I have used this site many times for writing transcriptions. You can pull the piano score into Finale and then move the lines around to where you want them to go for the particular group you are writing for."

I've learned much from listening to music, but I've learned the most from listening to music that I love—over and over again. Keep this idea in mind when you listen not only for analytical purposes but also for inspiration and enjoyment.

14 Pursue opportunities that appear.

Dr. Robert Gauldin was chairman of the composition department at the Eastman School of Music when I was a student there. During my sophomore or junior year—I can't remember which—I met with him and showed him some of my composition notebooks. I asked him if there was anything there, and if composition would be worth my pursuing. He considered my notebooks carefully and said he couldn't tell much from what's in a few notebooks and that I should take a few composition courses to see how things go.

That was excellent advice—excellent advice that I did not take. I admit that not taking his advice is one of my biggest regrets as a composer, but I have learned from this mistake. I follow opportunities now that are given to me, and I create my own opportunities. This mindset and action plan are now part of my continued learning and growing as a composer. Opportunities abound when you actively seek them. The next item includes ideas on how to create your own opportunities.

15   Ask, ask, ask.

In addition to pursuing opportunities, create your own. Ask for help and keep asking for help. Ask friends, teachers, and former teachers for help. We're often reluctant to ask for help or information because we're afraid of rejection, and we're hesitant to reveal what we don't know. Muster the courage to ask for things you need and want. Identify those who might have the answers AND ASK. Considering the worst that could happen—someone just says no—could embolden you to ask and keep asking for help. Even asking the wrong people often leads to their directing you to the right people. Think of all you can gain from asking all the right people all the right questions!

My recent switching from a Windows environment on my computers to Mac was a terrific example of "ask, ask, ask." I needed one heck of a lot of help with all aspects not only of working in the Mac OS X environment, but also in learning new aspects of my mainstay programs, MS Word, MS Excel, and Finale, and my learning to use other new Mac OS X apps. I posted my questions in online forums. I asked acquaintances who are familiar with Mac OS X a lot of questions. I live-chatted, phoned, and emailed questions to software vendors. Help, advice, and answers most often came quickly, much to my relief. Ask, ask, ask!

Composer Glenn Martin has also learned to ask, ask, ask. "When I was at NTSU (North Texas State University), I had asked then professor Rich Matteson that if a teaching opportunity ever appeared, I'd be interested. He eventually gave me a class to teach at NTSU, and called me to do workshops with him. Sometimes, you gotta ask!"

16 Equip yourself with the tools of the trade.

"Pictures at an Exhibition

Some of the equipment you may need includes a powerful computer, maybe a good external sound card, decent monitors and headphones, music notation software, sound libraries, a DAW (digital audio workstation), and perhaps a keyboard or a keyboard controller. I've used the music notation program Finale since the late 1990s. Other composers prefer Sibelius. Still others use Dorico, MuseScore, Notion, and LilyPond. There are other notation programs for PCs, laptops, and portables. See the "Resources" section for website addresses.

Composer Zander Hulme offers a caution on equipment. "There is no point buying middle-of-the-road tools," he says. "If you can't afford great gear, get the cheapest gear you can cope with using, and save up for great gear. The mentality of slowly climbing the gear ladder, progressing from item to item, is hugely wasteful and will cost you much more money in the end. I like to ask myself, 'if I had double the budget, would I still be considering buying the thing I'm considering now?'"

There are many choices available in hardware and software. If you are in school, or were in school, you probably use the same kind of equipment on which you learned in the classroom—mainly Sibelius or Finale, for notation software. If you're choosing hardware and software without having been school-trained, consider your needs and then get plenty of recommendations from composers whose work is similar to yours.

Composer Kim Diehnelt favors MuseScore. "Although I have used Sibelius when working for a music publisher, I have found that MuseScore works much the same," she says. "All my composing, printing, and publishing is done with MuseScore. I'm always delighted when musicians comment on how beautiful the manuscripts are."

For evaluating playback, composer Teresa O'Connell says, "I use my MacBook Air's internal speakers, headphones, or my Oontz Angle 3-Plus Portable Bluetooth Speaker."

Composer Ari Romppanen offers a useful insight into the tools of the trade for composing. "For me, the most important tools are pencils with erasers and paper," he says. "With them I feel free to do whatever I like. Any kind of technology helps in some way, but it can make barriers in other ways. For this reason, hardware and software can be a liability until you're proficient enough with it."

Composer Elizabeth Raum says, "I started using a notation program in the late 1990s, although I had written several operas and a great deal of music by hand," she says. "At first, I didn't think I could work with a computer because the requirement to work with something as mechanical as a computer was like trying to compose through remote control. However, eventually I was forced to figure it out because I had so much work to do. I knew I'd have to go beyond writing by hand and realized there were benefits to working with a computer, like copying and pasting, transposing, and extracting parts. It didn't take long for my brain to accept the computer as a piano substitute. Even now, however, I always print out what I write and play it on the piano because I need to feel the vibrations under my fingers to know it's right. I've worked with Finale on a Mac computer and use an Alesis Quadrasynth—old technology, I know, but I'm familiar with it."

Composer Jukka Viitasaari has modest software and hardware needs. "I use Sibelius, a MIDI keyboard, and my guitars," he says.

"I love notation software," says composer Mark Taylor. "There are ideas I get ('Hmmm… I think I want to repeat that section, but upside down and backwards and displaced by a sixteenth note…') that I would never use if I had to 'do the math' myself. Plus, even though I've worked as a copyist (and still do sometimes), I really hate copying parts. Furthermore, someone always loses or forgets a part at the last minute. If I have the score and parts in Dropbox as pdfs, I can just go to the nearest printer and make a new one. Other than that, I happen to love working with DAWs and sample libraries, especially for film and media work. Unless you happen to have an orchestra sitting around waiting for your next piece, a good DAW and some samples will allow you to write things other than a solo piece for whatever instrument you play. I use Sibelius as my notation software and Presonus Studio One as my DAW with instrument samples from Spitfire Audio, Output, and a few other companies."

"As a classical/romantic composer, I mainly use Finale, ProTools, and Audacity," says composer Laura Pettigrew. "I also use an iMac desktop computer, HP laptop, a Roland synthesizer, and a Yamaha keyboard."

Beware of becoming inundated in a sea of new gadgetry and software. From the examples above, choose a minimum of what you need to work. Then find a balance between staying aware of innovations and practicing your craft—composing! The "Resources" section includes hardware and software website addresses.

17 Ensure your work's professional appearance.

Learn proper music notation, and prepare manuscripts and parts conscientiously. Edit and proofread scores and parts diligently, or engage the services of a professional copyist.

This part of the publication process is vital, whether you self-publish your music or work with a publisher or publishers with whom you entered into contract agreement. Decades ago, publishers' sending me proof copies was more of a courtesy because staff editors proofread pieces. But these days, as publishing house staffs diminished to bare bones and music notation programs became the norm, composers are increasingly more responsible for editing and proofreading their work.

David Young, MD, produced a wonderful checklist for proofreading a musical score. He posted it originally on the old Finale forum about 12 years ago. You can download it here: https://forum.makemusic.com/attach.aspx/10230/Checklist.exp.3000.pdf. The Toronto Music Service also produced a score checklist, and you can find similar score proofreading checklists online.

Checklists aside, don't rely solely on proofreading your scores and parts with a checklist. Having your music performed is another excellent way to proofread the score and parts. You need to place the piece in the hands of a conscientious director who will be aware of—that is, hear—discrepancies in the score and parts, and who will alert the players to speak up if they spot suspicious items.

I most often include rehearsal and program notes with my pieces, so accurate text proofreading is as much a vital part of presenting a piece to publishers and performers as is proofreading scores and parts. Proofreading is a key to increasing credibility. Any music or text rife with errors causes readers to doubt your credibility, your message, and, ultimately, your music.

There's much more to proofreading text than checking for spelling and grammar errors. Before you proofread anything, choose a style. For example, will you write "1,000" or "1000"? "10:30 am" or 10:30 a.m."? "Employe" or "employee"? "Toward" or "towards"? Both choices in these examples are correct. The purpose of choosing a style is to maintain consistency in your text. That helps readers get through the material without stumbling over two items prepared in a different style (see item #22, "Gather a reference library"). I've found that some music publishers will likely accept the style you choose, as long as you apply that style consistently. Some publishers have their own styles for both music and text.

I've used mainly these three style manuals for text: *The Chicago Manual of Style*; *The Associated Press Stylebook*; and *The Elements of Style,* by William Strunk, Jr., and E. B. White.

Whichever style you choose, stick to it. In addition to preventing readers from stumbling over your words, readability and consistency are two important elements that keep readers interested.

With your style manual in one hand and your red pencil in the other, use these five practical ideas to increase your proofreading effectiveness for all the text you might write.

1 If several colleagues already proofread material, be sure that one step in the process includes someone's reading material aloud to another person who's checking what's read against the copy.

Even if you're by yourself for this process, read material aloud to yourself. When you read silently, you often correct errors automatically, so reading aloud helps you catch mistakes that you might otherwise overlook.

2 Record yourself reading a long document and then listen to the playback with the copy in hand. Mark mistakes you discover, and note areas you might want to smooth or rewrite. Hearing the material provides another perspective and lets you experience the material freshly. I've used Microsoft Word's "speak selected text" feature for this purpose. On my iMac, I enjoy using the Mac OS X Speech feature (Apple menu > System Preferences, click Accessibility, then click Speech). I highlight the text I want to hear and click Option-esc to begin the playback.

3 Don't depend solely on word-processing program spell checkers and grammar-checking options. They have their places, but using them isn't proofreading. Spell checkers overlook homophones (words that sound the same but are spelled differently, like their and there, here and hear, who's and whose, and principle and principal). Computer programs can't check facts, either, or ensure that important numbers, measure numbers, and other number references in your work are correct.

Do use spellcheckers and grammar checkers first. Then read the text backward, word for word, paragraph by paragraph. This technique lets you concentrate on spelling, not on the ideas that the words convey.

4 Verify all numbers. If you cite measure numbers, check the score or parts to make sure you're correct. That is, in program notes, for example, if you mention, say, the crescendo in measures 51-56, make sure the crescendo is actually in those measures.

5 Finally, effective proofreading ultimately translates into spending money wisely, so be sure all your proofing is accomplished before you send finalized materials to a printer or publisher. Publishers may charge extra for changing music and text during production stages. These changes become more costly as production continues.

Check a first proof that a publisher sends you very carefully—as if the proof were your own original and you're proofreading the entire package for the first time. Errors can creep in to works, especially when items are re-keyed manually or the music is notated again manually.

In addition, music needs to be proofread carefully after it's been copied from an XML file to a notation program that differs from your original submission—that is, a Finale file to Sibelius, or vice versa, for example.

Proofreading isn't a glamorous part of composing, but it can turn a performer or a publisher's skepticism into satisfaction and it can build performer and publisher confidence in your submissions. That's why proofreading is a vital part of the composing process. Proofreading can also transform reluctance into a heightened sense of your work's professional appearance and reliability. Ultimately, proofreading everything diligently helps you increase profits and visibility.

In addition to the score proofreading checklists mentioned above, Google "proofreading checklist" to find useful text proofreading resources.

I edit and proofread my music and writing mostly at the computer. But sometimes I like to edit and proofread my work elsewhere—in another room in my home, on the porch, at the library, in the park, sitting in bed before I go to sleep, at my car dealership during oil changes. Variety in my choosing these places inspires me and freshens my outlook on my work. I have no idea why, but a change in environment for proofreading text and music helps me concentrate and sharpens my work. It may help you, too.

18 Manage your time for your greatest advantage.

That's much easier said than done, and that's why all professionals are to some extent preoccupied with time management. This book is filled with a lot of suggestions—so much to do! Combine all these possible activities with changing priorities, family responsibilities, and unexpected needs, and you could easily become lost in a sea of conflicting commitments and desires.

For this reason, I accept that I need to make sacrifices, and that some things I'd like to do just will not get done—for now. For instance, I'd like to learn to become adept at using a DAW (digital audio workstation). I would also like to become skilled at using YouTube better, and I'd like to create a blog and be effective at blogging. But I've put these items lower on my priority list so that I can stay focused on composing music. Unfortunately, these goals will stay on my wish list for now—difficult choices that nonetheless have to be made. I will do these things, but just not now.

Composers' approaches to time management vary greatly, and it seems best to continually customize priorities as elements that demand our attention change. It's important to recognize when your time management works, when it's not working, and how to adjust.

Composer Laurie Jeanne Crockett says, "Instead of trying to compose and promote at the same time, it's best for me to have 'seasons' when I'm either composing or promoting. Overall, I spend 80 percent of my time composing and 20 percent promoting.

"'Seasons' refers to the times in which I'm either primarily composing or primarily promoting. However, since my Christmas disc was released, I do spend much of the holiday season managing Facebook posts and boosting them, and I usually spend very little time then composing. So in this respect I really do have a promotional 'season.' I'm always happy to have January roll around when everything slows down and I can squirrel away and spend weeks at the piano just coming up with new music."

Composer Rain Worthington practices another disciplined approach to time management: "I imagine that balancing time between composing and promotion is an ongoing struggle for most composers," she says. "While opportunities have opened up with self-publishing and the ever-changing music environment, a composer now also has to be a publicist, manager, and agent. It is often up to the individual composers to manage submissions and distribution of works; log performance notifications with the PROs (performance rights organization) for royalty credits; outreach to performers and music directors; and write and circulate press releases for concert and music news announcements. These tasks require a tremendous commitment of time, separate from composing, but they are necessary in the current music environment. The best way I have found to be able to secure time for composing is to choose simply NOT to turn on email or the Internet when my intention is to allot time to compose."

Composer Mark Taylor says, "I asked my wife to help me make a schedule for all the things I felt I needed to do every day, but we discovered that I either need seven more hours a day or we need to invent a couple of extra days a week to get it all in! I quickly figured out that I probably didn't need to do all those things every day and some of them were the same things with different names. I'm currently working on being much more consistent with finding and connecting with people who might be interested in my work by setting 'office hours' for business stuff. One day a week is prioritized for business, even though I do a little every day, and I make a very simple list (on a pad of paper on my desk) of a few things I need to get done. Once completed, I take a pen and cross them off. Crossing things off your list is enormously satisfying!"

Composer Grahame Gordon Innes keeps things simple. "I have a YouTube channel, which I advertise on Facebook and occasionally elsewhere, and I also have a website," he says. "I have a very clear way of balancing promoting with composing: I prioritize composing when I have ideas and inspiration. I promote myself only when time is available to do so."

Composer Alex Shapiro is both philosophical and practical in managing her time. "A working composer today wears enough professional hats to keep any milliner in business!," she says. "For most composers, the reality of a successful life in music is ironically one in which they spend more hours tending to the administrative responsibilities that keep all the wheels churning than they devote to the act of actually composing the next piece.

Adding to this irony is that the more successful the composer, the longer the lineup of commissions and looming deadlines. There seems to be no escaping the equation of 'more composing work equals less time in which to compose.'"

"My solution for finding a balance between the administrative and the creative parts of my career has been to look carefully at my insane schedule, cordon off a reasonable number of hours, or, ideally, consecutive days and nights, and mark them with a banner in my calendar as inviolable, sacrosanct, pure composing time. I make an appointment with my muses that I would no sooner break were it an appointment for any professional meeting. I've learned that unless we 'give' ourselves composing time, no one will give it to us, because day after busy day too readily becomes consumed by everything other than art-making."

"Even on the composing days, by necessity I still devote the morning to running my publishing business and keeping up with responsibilities that accompany my travel-intensive advocacy work as a speaker and board member of several organizations. I use a strict triage rule in which I answer only time-sensitive emails, and the rest are forced to make friends with each other for a few days crammed together in my inbox. Once lunchtime is over, I willfully switch gears, and re-enter the happy world of composing!"

Composer Laura Pettigrew's perspective on managing her time is both amazing and instructive. "As a self-employed composer and single mother, with my first education in nursing, I returned to college at age 37, raising and supporting my two sons, then ages four and 10, to pursue and receive my B.Mus. in flute performance and composition and M. Mus. in composition," she says. "Having to balance the needs of my sons' health, welfare, and education, including involvement in music and sports, in addition to carrying a full load of classes and commitment to performance, a fulltime job, two part-time jobs and a studio of 40 private students, was in and of itself a balancing act. I've learned just to adapt to achieve balance. That remains true managing time to promote my work and to compose. With this kind of time management, it is vitally important to recognize that we are human, to prioritize, maintain a schedule, not over extend ourselves, and maintain our physical and mental health."

19 Set goals and measure progress.

Time management requires having goals so that you can prioritize your tasks and activities. I set goals, usually a few each year. I write them down and then list actions that will help me meet my goals. I consult my goals and actions list often, adding, changing, and removing items, and checking off and replacing tasks I've completed. I review my goals about every year.

When I achieve a goal, I consider which actions led to that success. If I fall short of meeting a goal, I review my action plan and, if I deem that goal still worthy, I change my action plan with better success in mind.

During the last few years, my goals have included establishing a Facebook composer page, setting up a YouTube channel, establishing a LinkedIn presence, and setting target numbers and kinds of Facebook friendships and LinkedIn connections. Last year, one of my main goals was to move from a Windows computer environment to a Mac OS X environment. My current annual goals include composing or completing four or five pieces (I don't compose quickly), placing them on my YouTube channel, securing premier performances of two or three of those pieces, and submitting them for publication.

Setting goals, having an action plan, and taking steps to meet my goals helps me in several ways. Meeting goals gives me a sense of accomplishment and personal satisfaction. Having a plan and tasks at hand, large and small, help guard against procrastination. Along these lines, articulating goals and the steps to take to reach them helps me be more productive and make smarter decisions and more focused choices. Periodically evaluating my goals and action plan helps me identify opportunities I may not have seen before.

The internet is loaded with helpful sites that can assist you in setting and reaching goals. If you don't already write down goals and create an action plan to reach them, I recommend you do so.

Composer Laurie Jeanne Crockett says, "I set goals because they are motivating. My goals range from daily goals that I write on my 'to-do' list, to long-range goals that are a few months out to as far out as five years (the 'where do you see yourself?' question.) One point here: You benefit from long-range goals by breaking them down into smaller goals. My goals have also changed over time as my music has changed, as my knowledge of the business has changed, and as life circumstances have changed, so it's good to be flexible.

"It seems simple, but I measure my progress by actually accomplishing set goals. It's easy to talk about doing something, but eventually you just have to do it, whatever that 'it' is for you—whether it's calling people to collaborate on a project, setting a date for a performance, setting up a Facebook page, getting into the recording studio, etc. The more goals you actually accomplish, the more you will eventually find yourself moving forward."

20 Take local college courses (or audit them), adult school classes, summer school offerings, and community enrichment programs.

These offerings typically include business-related courses, computer classes, music theory courses, and perhaps ensembles. Check your school district, township, and county government for course offerings. You can often find flyers and brochures on these offerings at your local library and community center, or online.

21 Get a library card.

Become familiar with your library's offerings and services. Most libraries can get you just about any book on, if necessary, inter-library loan. So just about any reference book you might want to consult can be available this way. When your local library secures an inter-library loan for you, it is most often free, but obtaining the book can take weeks. A book on brass band instrumentation I borrowed took three weeks to arrive at my library, and a music theory book I wanted to read took about a month to arrive. Still, this service is valuable—just remember it isn't usually fast.

22 Gather a reference library.

My music references include *The Harvard Dictionary of Music*, Persichetti's *Twentieth Century Harmony*, Elaine Gould's *Behind Bars: The Definitive Guide to Music Notation*, and Gardner Read's *Music Notation*. I also use several online music dictionaries, and I have a score library consisting mostly of my favorite pieces, which I consult often.

Composer Paolo Fradiani references include *The Study of Orchestration*, by Samuel Adler, *Treatise on Counterpoint and Fugue*, by Theodore Dubois (in French with only an Italian translation—not in English), and, he says, "Arnold Schoenberg's books on form, harmony, counterpoint, and composition."

Composer Christopher Carlone also recommends Samuel Adler's *The Study of Orchestration*. "It was probably the most beneficial text I ever acquired in college," he says.

Composer Michael J. Miller suggests Mark Camphouse's book *Conductors on Composing for Band*. "It's a phenomenal book and gives an indepth look into some great composers," he says.

Composer Mike Hall suggests *Modern Recording Techniques* by Huber & Runstein.

Composer Laurie Jeanne Crockett says, "My music references include Alfred's *Essentials of Music Theory: Complete*, by Andrew Surmani, Karen Farnum Surmani, and Morton Manus, and *The Complete Idiot's Guide to Music Theory*, by Michael Miller."

Composer Rain Worthington says, "Having not taken an academic path to composition, as a self-taught composer, I go to lots of YouTube videos to learn about instrument techniques. These videos are great because they provide the real sound of the technique effect. There are videos for everything that often feature wonderfully masterful musicians. So a typical search on YouTube, WikiHow, or Quora might be, "what is the difference between portamento and glissando?" I also have appreciated educational sites, like Don Freud's "Instrument Studies for Eyes and Ears," http://resources.music.indiana.edu/isfee/, and Philharmonia Orchestra's site: http://www.philharmonia.co.uk/explore/instruments."

Composer Tony Tester recommends several references: "*Orchestration* by Joseph Wagner, my constant companion, and *Orchestration* by Cecil Forsyth; *Hearing and Writing Music* by Ron Gorow—this book is wonderful for looking at melodic lines and rhythmic themes in an alternative and quirky fashion; *Writing Better Lyrics* by Pat Patterson, a perennial favorite because it logically approaches techniques for writing better lyrics; and *Arranging Music for the Real World* by Vince Corozine. This book is a must for the crossover between classical and jazz approaches to scoring and arranging."

"I still refer to Walter Piston's *Orchestration* and *Practical Vocabulary of Music in English, French, German, and Italian* to select the best musical terms," says Composer Kim Diehnelt. "Most importantly, though, I refer to scores. For example, I recently wrote for full orchestra and wanted to review how to capture certain trombone and low brass qualities. There were specific spots in some of Bruckner's symphonies that I thought had the color and texture I was considering. I consult the 'experts' via their scores.

"For big-picture concepts and new perspectives, I like reaching into other fields. I have found reading about the work of playwrights to be very helpful. My favorite is *The Art of Dramatic Writing*, by Lajos Egri. I also find it helpful to explore concepts of narrative in, for instance, *The Situation and the Story: The Art of Personal Narrative* by Vivian Gornick."

Composer Glenn Martin suggests Abebooks.com if you want to obtain some references. "It is a national association of used book stores," he says. "I have found rare books on Abebooks.com that were listed for hundreds of dollars for pennies (used and out of print) on other sites. Sometimes, Abe is the only place I can find a book."

Composer R. Duane Hendricks says, "My reference library includes many books written by composers, such as *The Shaping Forces of Music*, by Ernst Toch, *Music and Imagination*, by Aaron Copland, *Themes and Conclusions*, by Igor Stravinsky, and *Findings*, by Leonard Bernstein."

Composer Divan Gattamorta says, "Here in Brazil, I most often consult *Rítmica* by José Eduardo Gramani, *Arranjo* by Carlos Almada, *Harmonia Funcional* by Carlos Almada, *Harmonia* by Paulo José de Siqueira Tiné, and *A Arte de Compor Música para o Cinema* by Eugênio Matos."

For my writing text, I consult the *The Chicago Manual of Style*, *Associated Press Stylebook and Libel Manual*, *The Elements of Style*, and *Words Into Type*. I also own a hard-copy Webster's *New Collegiate Dictionary*, Merriam-Webster's *Collegiate Dictionary*, *The Doubleday Roget's Thesaurus in Dictionary Form*, and J. I. Rodale's *The Synonym Finder*, but I admit I haven't opened these books in years—now I use Microsoft Word's Thesaurus, dictionary.com, and thesaurus.com.

Check out recommended reference books from the library. If they meet your needs as references, buy used books online to save money. You could also post a note in Facebook forums and other forums to see if anyone might sell a reference book to you. See the "Resources" section for more reference suggestions.

23 Attend live concerts of the kinds of music you compose.

Attending live performances regularly can help you learn trends of which musical styles directors are programming for performance. In addition, I find attending live performances so inspirational, I almost always leave conjuring up new ideas. In addition, search online and on YouTube for these kinds of performances.

You might also attend rehearsals if the cost of concert tickets is too high. Always ask the conductor for permission first, though.

24 Join a performing rights society.

I'm an ASCAP member. Joining a performing rights society can help identify you as a professional because you'd note it near your composer name on your scores and parts. A performing rights society can also help you reap performance royalties. Licensing organizations also provide workshops, networking opportunities, instrument and health insurance, marketing assistance, and merchandise purchase discounts. Find organization website addresses in the "Resources" section.

Composer Rain Worthington adds, "Registering as both a writer and a publisher has been very useful in generating the small amounts of royalty income from performances of my music."

25 Join professional organizations and internet forums, and attend conferences.

Because my focus is mainly educational music, I am a member of the National Association for Music Education, the Florida Music Educators Association, and ASCAP. There are many groups and associations for like-minded composers. Investigate them, ask for recommendations on them, and if they benefit you, join. And when you become a member, do list your membership as part of your biographical information.

Similarly, groups and organizations to which you belong might offer enrichment programs. Watch for these kinds of opportunities, and take professional development workshops covering such topics as contracts, promotion, score preparation and publishing, engraving, copyright and commissioning agreements, and other career essentials. You can also find a wealth of these kinds of resources online.

Composer Ronald J. Brown says that organization membership can create performance opportunities. "I have been a member of the Delian Society for many years," he says. "Members have group projects in which I have always participated, and as a result, some of my short works have been performed in France,

Japan, Seattle, and Costa Rica, giving me contact and exposure to musicians around the world."

26 Network effectively.

"**N**etworking" means meeting others in person and online. It means making yourself and your goals visible to others. It means helping others with your expertise, and seeking help with your questions and concerns. Expand your support network by becoming a networking superstar.

Composer Alex Shapiro says, "Networking is a somewhat shallow term for what the music business is all about: building relationships. Genuine connections between people can be created in pixels and in person, and being active in both intersecting worlds can be very rewarding."

She offers excellent advice in four specific networking avenues:

- "Attend concerts, and especially those that include the music of living composers," she says. "Say hello to the performers afterward, and they might even invite you to join them for a post-gig beverage. Avoid the urge to hand anyone a CD, flash drive, or score on the spot, and instead, focus on enjoying everyone's company. The next day is a great time to follow up with a friendly, personal

email (NEVER a bulk mailing) and you can include a website link— especially one to a specific piece or event that might be of particular interest to that musician."
- "Attend music conferences: No matter what kind of music you compose, there's a conference somewhere in the world that's dedicated to it," she says. "Two or three intense days and evenings of clinics and concerts can often be the entry ticket to many opportunities. Armed with business cards and CDs or thumb drives to hand out, walk the aisles and engage with people at the booths, go to the workshops and chat with the participants afterward, and participate in social events." See the next item for more information on getting the most from conferences.
- "Participate in interactive online communities: Avoid posting too often solely about yourself, in favor of posting things geared toward a broader swath of other people's interests," she says.
- "Get involved with music advocacy organizations: Join national and international groups and be engaged with them online, and become active with local groups," she says. "There is a wealth of knowledge, camaraderie, and potential opportunity to be had through the joy of volunteerism and improving the scene for one's peers, whether or not one's already established."

I maintain an increasingly active networking presence on Facebook and on LinkedIn. On Facebook, I posted a short description of an easy concert band piece I wrote with a link to the score and playback on my YouTube channel. I routinely post these kinds of notes. A publisher saw one of these posts, listened to the music, and offered to publish the piece. Similarly, I've secured readings of many works through Facebook and LinkedIn, and several performances and premiers.

Composer Mark Taylor takes a wide view of networking. "One of my mentors, Max Roach, used to tell me to 'be on the scene,'" he says. "Go to stuff. Go to lots of stuff! Hear music, see plays, watch dancers, go to screenings, etc. When you find a community you want to be involved in, make yourself useful. Volunteer for stuff and get to know everyone. Networking isn't always linear. Sometimes what you get back comes two or three times removed from the people you put things out to. Make friends. You're building relationships, not looking for work. Also, people like to work with people they like, so be nice. There are digital ways to do all of this as well, and you can cover a huge geographical area getting to know people online. Shared interests are a fantastic ice breaker."

27 Apply conference skills.

Conferences at national, regional, state, and local levels are excellent opportunities to network by meeting new colleagues, contacts, and clients; identify trends; discover software innovations and improvements in computer music applications; and gain inspiration. Use these five ideas to make the most of conferences and seminars.

1 Even though conference registration materials may include a useful tote, I sometimes bring a backpack or a cloth totebag for holding free materials and samples. Some vendors include totebags as giveaways.

2 My iPhone notes, voice memos, and camera apps get a vigorous workout at conferences because I take pictures and make notes on my smartphone of everything I want to remember when I get home. Add your name to mail and email lists for product information, and bring plenty of business cards. Pass them out liberally.

3 Exhibitors are often experts in using their products, and they can provide practical guidance on their wares. To talk shop with exhibitors or to consult them on specific product questions, identify slower times for them when they are more likely to be able to help you with fewer distractions. Mornings are usually best if you need to discuss a product at some length. Make an appointment if you need more time.

4 Call me old school, but I believe one's professional appearance is important, not only when you attend conferences, exhibits, and shows, but also when you meet in person with clients and publishers. Professional attire isn't strictly necessary, but do appear neat. I avoid sneakers, jeans, tee shirts, and golf shirts. I call my attire at most conferences "casual professional"—Shirt, slacks, and comfortable shoes. Comfortable shoes are a must because conference venues don't often have many places just to sit and rest.

Composer Zander Hulme offers a tip on professional appearance. "In some creative fields, having a high standard of personal presentation will not only establish you as serious about your work, but may even help you stand out," he says. "Working in the games industry, the vast majority of my colleagues and the people I meet all wear t-shirts. My being 'the guy who always wears a bow tie' has made me easily memorable and identifiable at industry events."

5 During a conference, my creativity and inspiration often shift into high gear. I remain ready at all times to record ideas on my iPhone.

28 Promote yourself on social media and get your works performed, published, viewed, or purchased.

This strategy can keep your name "out there," and it lets readers get to know you a bit better. For one thing, on my Facebook composer page and on my LinkedIn feed I post questions about all things musical. I craft questions and topics for discussion to make them stimulating, "meaty," intellectual, inviting, and sincere. I try to invite participation and engage readers with thoughts and questions that genuinely concern me. I respond to others' questions and comments, too. I also use hashtags on my LinkedIn posts, a new LinkedIn feature.

I also post news about premiers of my works, new published music, and awards and honors I've garnered, and when I finish a work and post it on my YouTube channel. I also solicit performances and recordings on Facebook, YouTube, and LinkedIn.

Creating vibrant posts that work

Crafting posts that work on social media is an art. Before you write anything, decide the purpose of your post. Craft your post based on a clear vision of what you want it to accomplish. When you create your post, get to the point. You want to ensnare the reader right away! Don't try to be cute—that causes readers to roll their eyes and run away as fast as they can. Be terse, choose your words carefully, say what you want—and not one word more. Stay in the active voice—it's more powerful and less wordy than passive voice. Adding a photo can be helpful, but if you do, make sure it's relevant. Don't provide an email address in public posts—just say, "PM me," "Message me," or something similar. If you ask for something, add "Thank you" or "Thanks" at the end of your post.

When I invite someone to friend me on Facebook or connect with me on LinkedIn, I scan their Facebook pages, bios, and websites, if they have them. I've contacted some of these "friends" directly, asking them to perform and record various pieces. My aim is to acquire good recordings of my works so that I can send the recordings with scores for publication consideration. I highlight the idea that polishing and performing one of my pieces can be a beneficial educational opportunity for students. If I get a good recording and submit it to a publisher, I mention that I'd add a dedication to the group and to the conductor on the score. Here is one such solicitation:

As a composer, I seek recordings of my music's performances to send with scores to my publishers. For this reason, I thought it might be a fun and educational opportunity for your students to rehearse, perform, and record a piece I've recently completed: "[Piece Title]" a Grade [difficulty level], [ensemble type] work.

My publishers greatly prefer recordings of live performances over midi renderings. They then use these recordings to promote the sheet music. If you can provide such a recording of this piece and if I submit it to one of my publishers, I'd be happy to include a dedication on the score to your group and to you as its director. I do know the effort these projects entail, so I'm hoping you agree this might be a good experience for the kids. I have not set a deadline yet for this project.

May I email you the score, mp3 file, and my director rehearsal, performance, and program notes for your perusal?

My track record with this solicitation has been good enough to garner several recordings of pieces that I've submitted for publication. Many band directors, from elementary school through college and professional organizations, agree that this experience would benefit the kids, and some directors take me up on the offer. Some don't, though, and for a variety of entirely legitimate reasons, so I'm not deterred when I get a "no."

Bands have recorded several of my pieces over a few years, and in one case, that led to an offer for a semester as a composer in residence (which I could not take because I was relocating) and several commissions (which I did complete).

I've posted similar items on Facebook and LinkedIn, each with a slightly different purpose. First, I like to announce premiers of my works because they generate interest and can lead to publication:

My concert band piece "Mythical Royals and Their Heroic Defenders," will be premiered by the Cypress Symphonic Band (Houston, TX) during its 2017-18 season. The piece is one of four winning works selected for performance in a juried competition. Follow the score and listen here: https://www.youtube.com/watch?v=krv3FthAZPQ&feature=youtu.be.

This kind of post garners interest and credibility in my work because the kudos come not from me but from someone else:

"Euphotrombotonia" features a concert band's euphonium, trombone, and baritone players. This power-packed Grade 3 piece is a little quirky and a little different—and a lot of spirited fun for players and audiences. Follow the score and listen here: https://www.youtube.com/watch?v=4bO51iv4dmA. "Euphotrombotonia" was named a winner in the 3rd Annual Sul Ross State University (Texas, USA) Wind Ensemble Composition Contest. If you like this work, please do like my Facebook page. Contact me if you're interested in performing this piece. Thanks!

"Euphotrombotonia" has since been published by Bell Music Publishing.

These announcements and solicitations can create an opportunity for directors to recommend your music to publishers, or publishers themselves to hear your music and follow scores. I've received offers for publication for several pieces this way. For instance, I posted a note on my Facebook page about a new piece, "Bluesy Chalumeau Cha-Cha," that I had posted on my YouTube channel. This post led to a publishing offer and publication by Alry Publications.

In addition, as a result of my posting this kind of announcement, I've received invitations from publishers to submit music for publication consideration.

Furthermore, when a publisher releases one of my works, I usually post this kind of announcement:

My concert band arrangement of the "Kyrie" from Mozart's "Requiem," my concert band piece "Copycat's Convoy," and another concert band piece, "Little Concert Overture with Fanfare" are now published by PDFbandmusic.com. To purchase this music, visit https://pdfbandmusic.com/search?type=product&q=michaels.

Composer Laurie Jeanne Crockett uses Facebook and social media differently. "I attract people to my YouTube channel mostly by boosting songs via Facebook," she says. "One thing I have uploaded on my channel is a Christmas album I did some years ago, in which I arranged several lesser known European Christmas carols from the 17th and 18th centuries. So some of my YouTube views are actually generated by YouTube searches for some of these older carols. This has created an obscure niche that brings people organically, and it consistently increases traffic between November and December.

"Boosting on Facebook requires a Facebook page, which is different from just the regular Facebook account. It's a really easy way to do a little bit of marketing. It doesn't cost any money to create a page, and there are some useful YouTube tutorials that explain how to set up a Facebook page. The advantage of a Facebook page is that it allows you to 'boost' content that you have added to your page from Youtube or from other social media sites. 'Boosting' is basically paid advertising, and again, there are really good tutorials on Youtube that explain the boosting process. You first have to upload your songs onto your Youtube channel, then 'share' them from Youtube to your Facebook page. Facebook will then give you the option to boost your post. You can choose the age, location, and interests of your target audience, the number of days the boost will run, and how much you want to spend on the ad."

Another idea for promoting yourself and your work, even if roundabout, is to write articles for local, state, regional, national, and association publications. I first started contributing articles to state music education magazines, after which I began contributing to *The Instrumentalist*. I wrote so much for these entities that I eventually served brief stints as an associate editor at *The Instrumentalist* and managing editor of *Music Educators Journal*.

Nevertheless, writing for magazines this way is a good way to place your name and work in front of directors who would choose to perform your music, engage you as a clinician, or commission you to compose a work. I wrote mostly how-to articles and insightful pieces designed to be informative, helpful, or inspirational. I based these pieces on my teaching experience.

Composer Ari Romppanen is also a writer. "I've written several articles for composers' magazines and for my own web page," he says. "Writing helps me clarify my thoughts, so it is useful for me, even if nobody ever reads them. Every now and then I'm asked for new material."

29 Create a website to increase your exposure and sell your music.

I maintain two websites: One on Facebook (https://www.facebook.com/composerarthurjmichaels) and one on YouTube (https://www.youtube.com/channel/UC95zzUgP6liWA_ozo7oQPCQ). However, if I were selling my own music, I would also create a separate website for this purpose.

"I have both a professional website and a YouTube channel, which I believe are essentials for any composer," says composer Rain Worthington. "Your professional website is your professional home. And while current social media sites such as Facebook, Twitter, and Instagram can generate some interest in one's music, YouTube has proven to be one of the best 'go-to' resources for people to discover new music. I also use SoundCloud's option for private links to send audio tracks when submitting scores."

In addition, on your website or Facebook page include your resume and keep it up to date. Place some current, complementary photographs of you there, too, and perhaps one formal portrait of yourself. In the "Resources" section, peruse the websites of this book's contributors to see the information they've included and how they have organized this information.

30 Build a YouTube channel.

I prefer to submit music scores for publication with recordings of live performances, and YouTube videos help me solicit groups to perform and record these pieces. The "videos" I place on my YouTube channel are my scores, page by page, synced to the playback recordings. I create pithy, bright announcements of my placing a piece on my YouTube channel, which I post on my Facebook composer page. I then share those announcements in appropriate Facebook newsgroups and pages, and I invite ensemble directors to view them. My strategy is to solicit ensemble directors to perform and record my music so that I can submit live recordings to publishers with the scores. I've also received publication and performance offers directly from this strategy. Even if my postings don't lead to my obtaining a polished recording, posting my works on YouTube can garner interest in my music and attract performers to my works.

I've organized my YouTube channel in playlists of my concert band music, choral music, string orchestra music, and ensemble music. Each video includes the page-by-page scrolling score and the audio playback synced to the page turns. In my descriptions of each video, I include excerpts from my conductor notes and some promotional text.

There are many ways to post audio with scores to create a YouTube video. These instructions pertain to creating a video in Windows. However, on my iMac, I've recently been doing the same thing in iMovie. There is much more complicated and expensive movie-making software available both for Windows and Mac OS, but I chose what was for me convenient and least expensive for my needs.

Nevertheless, to post my scores and audio in a Windows environment, I followed these 11 steps:

1 I write a terse, informative, and alluring description of the piece. All or some of this text will appear as the piece's description on my YouTube channel. I often spend days honing this description because it has to draw readers in fast and get them to listen to the piece. This item is the brief description of the piece that viewers see when they bring up one of my YouTube playlists.

2 I create a list of keywords that I will include with the piece when I upload it to my YouTube channel. Get help with keywords from YouTube's analytics websites and tutorials—it's very important. Visit https://www.youtube.com/analytics for help. Keywords, the words or phrases that Google searchers use to land on your music, may surprise you, so it's important to get them right. For all this, you first need a Google or YouTube account—Google owns YouTube.

3 Then on my desktop PC I create a folder called "Assets - [piece title]," into which I will place all the files necessary for the YouTube item.

4 After I make the playback in Finale as good as I can get it, I export a WAV file of the piece—I read somewhere that WAV files and aiff files work better on YouTube than mp3s, so all my YouTube audio files are WAVs. For exporting audio in Finale, I usually add a blank measure at the beginning and end of the piece because Finale begins and cuts off the music too abruptly.

5 Finale volume is usually way too soft, so after I export the WAV file or aiff from Finale, I import it into Audacity (http://www.audacityteam.org/), trim the beginning and end just a tad, and normalize the entire file to -.05 dB. In Audacity, "normalize" is a dropdown menu item under "Effect." When you click on "Normalize...," the dropdown menu that appears lets you choose or write in the maximum normalization amplitude. I then save and place this audio file into my project assets folder.

6 After I have primped and preened the score with meticulous editing, I save each score page as an individual PDF file in the assets folder. For example, those files, score page by score page, will include 01[piece title].pdf, 02[piece title].pdf, 03[piece title].pdf, etc.

I've seen other composers' websites and sample scores, and some of them use a watermark. I've recently begun to place a watermark on my score page PDFs. I use a simple "for perusal only." Of course, centered at the bottom of each piece's first page I place this copyright notice, with the current year:

© 2020 Arthur J. Michaels

All Rights Reserved.

7 After I've saved all the score pages as individual PDFs, I bring them all into http://pdf2png.com/. Before uploading page files here, choose the tab "PDF to PNG." I then save each uploaded PDF page as a PNG file. Then I move these PNG files into the project assets folder.

Saving the PDF pages as PNGs is unnecessary in Mac, because iMovie can use PDFs. Now that I work in iMovie on a Mac, I no longer need to save the PDFs as PNGs.

8 Then I create a custom thumbnail for the piece. Look at all my YouTube pieces and you can see that each one has a custom thumbnail. I think that's important for product recognition and consistency. To create the thumbnail, I condense the piece's first score page temporarily (I don't save it). This temporary move usually requires my moving staffs and text closer together. I create PNG files of the condensed first score page (usually just the first few measures of the first few staff lines) and the title. I then bring these files into my account at https://www.canva.com/ (an account is free). I also use one of the free YouTube logos in Canva. I create the custom header there as a 1920x1080 PNG. After downloading the PNG thumbnail to my desktop, it then goes into the piece's assets folder.

I've recently begun to use photographs as thumbnails. Photographs are dramatic and encourage directors to listen and follow scores, far more than condensed score thumbnails. I use photographs from sites that offer free images, like pexels.com. I credit the photographer on the thumbnail.

9 In MS Word I create a title PNG. I used to place annotations at the end of my videos, directing viewers to click on my playlists to hear more music and view more scores. YouTube phased out annotations, so my newest YouTube videos include a card somewhere in the video with a similar message.

10 I then open Windows Movie Maker (WMM) in Windows 10 and create a new project with the piece's name as the title. I use an older version of WMM—version 6, from the Windows XP days. It has a timeline that I like to use, and I haven't found the timeline in newer WMM versions. I chose WMM 6 because it's free and easy to use.

11 I then create the "movie." The trick is to sync the page appearances and page turns with the audio file. It takes practice, but once you get the hang of it, the task goes faster. This work is very similar in WMM and in iMovie.

I'm getting more involved in YouTube analytics now. I can't offer any useful advice here except to say that I'm learning more about analyzing how people view my videos. I keep track of my videos in YouTube analytics.

This process may seem more complicated and cumbersome than it actually is because I've detailed it in a step-by-step fashion. Others surely have different procedures with different software. In fact, to create "movies" of your music scores with audio playback, Google "screen capture software" to find a wealth of free and paid software for Windows and Mac OS X.

Composer Raymond Burkhart also has a YouTube channel that's geared toward self-publishing. "I have a YouTube channel: https://www.youtube.com/user/RaymondBurkhartPhD: in addition to my blog and website," he says. "I also have both personal and 'band' Facebook pages and both Twitter and LinkedIn pages. I haven't found Instagram or other social media to be very helpful to me, but composers of other kinds of music might find them essential. The idea is to inform the public about commissions, publications, performances, and appearances, using Facebook and Twitter to point them to other sites, my own site, my blog, and my YouTube channel. Because I self-publish, it's essential to get the word out and provide links to where potential customers can order my music or inquire about commissions. It takes untold amounts of time, and sometimes lots of money, to build, maintain, and update a website, and I do this in addition to the time it takes to compose, be a teacher and performer and scholar, and publish and sell my music."

31 Start a blog.

I do not have a blog. However, some composers have them, especially those who self-publish. By way of their blogs, they maintain an active, engaged audience. A blog is something you might consider because blogging can increase your visibility, help promote and sell your works, and draw more hits on search engines with keen use of keywords.

Composer Raymond Burkhart does have a blog, "but I don't blog a lot, and I blog now less frequently than in the first few years," he says. "My plan was to write much more often, on topics that might interest others and sometimes draw attention to my published music. So I've written about musicians I've known, composers worthy of note, my own commissions and premieres, topics relating to brass chamber music (a specialty of mine), things I just find funny, a little bit of music criticism, and other topics. To let my blog be known, there is a prominent link in my website's primary navigation, and after I've blogged, I post about it to social media. My blog: http://raymondburkhartphd.blogspot.com/. My website: https://raymondburkhart.com/news/.

32 Study the market.

Whether or not publication is one of your goals, study the music of other composers in your genre. One way to study the market is to be in a position to evaluate the flow of materials to the publisher. You could work in the industry as a copyist or editor, become an intern in the industry, or work in publishing in some other supportive role.

I was a magazine editor and writer for many years, so I regularly evaluated queries and manuscripts. I saw regularly what others were thinking and doing, and through the inspiration that view provided, I applied the best of what I saw to my own work.

You don't have to be in such a position to review the work of others. There are plenty of showcase websites and online forums you can visit to review others' music.

As a composer, though, I've never held a position with a publisher. However, identifying publishing trends helps greatly in composing salable music. Studying the market can also help you decide in which publisher catalogs your music might fit best. Here's how I study the market.

- Ask publishers if there is a best "season" or time during which they prefer to review materials. Some publishers review material year-round. Others review material several times annually. Some publishers review music for publication during one period of several months. Some publishers explain their review practices on their websites. If you're interested in a publisher that doesn't explain its review strategy, always ask about a submission's timing.
- Before the advent of the internet, most publishers produced recordings of new materials with study scores for director evaluation. These days, some publishers still produce CDs and study scores for review, and other publishers use their websites for this purpose. Publisher websites and their review packages are another source for studying the market. Publishers who produce CDs and study scores often distribute these promotional items at conferences and trade shows.
- Look at the scoring. At various grade levels of concert band music, for instance, how many flute, clarinet, saxophone, trumpet, F horn, trombone, and percussion parts do the scores include? Do the staffs include divided notes? Does the publisher produce full scores even for the easiest concert band music? Does the publisher produce condensed conductor scores? In string music, does the publisher include a 3rd violin/viola treble clef staff in the score?

Consider also the score's instrumentation, layout, typefaces, and margins. These items can help you create, or re-create, scores for submissions to publishers. Some publishers maintain a specific style for scores and parts for instrumentation, layout, typefaces, positioning on the page, and margins, for example. In these cases, I've sometimes reworked my scores according to a publisher's most frequent scoring style for various grade levels of music because the less editing your score requires, the more attractive is your submission.

For instance, does the publisher call it string bass, bass, double bass, or contrabass? If the publisher is consistent with a naming convention, rename your instruments in your score for submission accordingly. Check all other score elements this way and apply the publisher's style to your submission.

- I also scan a publisher's music titles. Are they safe and stodgy? Playful and fun? Odd and unusual? Titles can help you decide if your music fits in to a publisher's offerings.
- Learn all you can about how a publisher promotes the sale of its sheet music. How did you discover the publisher? Does the publisher regularly attend trade shows and exhibit at educational conferences and venues? You can ask publisher representatives these questions directly at shows and conferences that you attend. Sometimes publishers list on their websites the shows and promotional appearances they make.
- Some publishers include instrument range charts on their websites that spell out the difficulty levels of many musical qualities for each grade level of music they publish. These charts can be a useful guide in your composing by themselves, but if a publisher includes this kind of chart on its website, make sure your submitted composition adheres to these guidelines.
- With your market study well underway, you can begin to think about submitting music for publication.

33 How to submit music for publication consideration.

Composer Jukka Viitasaari encapsulates good advice: "You need an MP3 file with NotePerformer sounds, and Sibelius files or PDFs," he says. "Your submission has to be well-edited."

One of my final steps to submitting a piece for publication consideration is to perform a special kind of editing. I print the score two pages per landscaped sheet. Then I tape the pages together and lay them out so that I can see the entire piece in front of me. I then play back the work several times, listening to the orchestration. This step provides a visual perspective on the piece. I can see in the score where I might thin out the score, or beef it up, or change some of the doubling to alter the mood and fill it with more variety and interest. As I listen to the piece this way, usually several times, I circle places in the score that need my attention, and I'll write brief reminders in the score on what I might change.

After I make these changes, if any, I'm ready to find a home for the piece with a publisher. Consider this step-by-step guide to submitting music for publication consideration. Before submitting material for publication, review "Study the Market," item #32. Submission policies among publishers in different genres, and even publishers in the same genre, have varying requirements. Follow these nine steps, but adapt them to your needs and to publishers' requirements.

1 Perform initial tasks in this process online. You'll want to match the kind of music you compose with the kind of music publishers offer. You want close matches here—don't submit material that's very different from the kind of music a publisher offers. Visit publisher websites and consider their catalogs, how often they come out with new material, their list of composers, any "about us" or "who we are" information, and, most importantly if they're offered, their submission guidelines.

2 Based on the previous step, create a list of publishers to whom you'd like to submit material—that is, publishers who publish the kind of music you compose. You can order your list according to your assessment of a publisher's efforts to promote their catalog offerings, which venues and how many events they attend to promote music, and their reputation.

3 Some publishers provide detailed submission guidelines. If submission guidelines are available, follow them to the letter—no skimping.

4 If you don't see submission guidelines on a publisher's website, query via email or through the publisher's messaging form. In most cases, you will get a response. You'd mention the piece or pieces you'd like to send, the instrumentation, difficulty level, and duration. If the publisher wants email submissions, mention the files you'd submit. If the publisher wants only hard-copy submissions by regular mail, mention which documents you'd send with a CD recording of the piece—for instance, the PDF score, mp3 playback file, and any conductor and performance notes you've written. I also like to mention that the score was created in Finale when a publisher to whom I'm submitting says that they accept only Finale files.

Here's an example of one of my submission queries.

Dear Xxxxxxx: For publication consideration I'd like to send "Brassy Capriccio," a moderately difficult original work for brass quintet. I can email the PDF full score (created in Finale), mp3 playback file, and my PDF director/program notes. The playback file of this piece is a recording by Flower City Brass, a brass quintet of graduate students at the Eastman School of Music. May I email these materials?

If the publisher says it does not review unsolicited submissions, either in an email response or on its website, move on.

5 When you get the go-ahead, send exactly what you proposed. That's why my submission introductory letters mimic my queries (see step 7, below).

6 Don't make multiple submissions to different publishers. It's tempting to do so, I know, but you could burn a bridge if both publishers accept a piece and you have to withdraw a work from consideration.

7 Whether you submit via email or regular mail, your submission package has to be nothing short of thoroughly professional. If you have printed stationery—and you should—use it to write your introductory letter. In your letter, include the items mentioned in your query and a short biographical paragraph.

Here's one of my email submission letters:

Attached herewith are the scores and mp3 files for "Sanctus," for SATB a cappella choir, and "Hymn of Peace," for SA or SAB chorus with piano and optional flute accompaniment. Attached also are a very brief bio and publications list.

The recording of "Sanctus" is my Finale playback with choir "aahs." The recording of "Hymn of Peace" is a performance by the Duquesne University (Pittsburgh, PA) Chamber Singers, directed by Dr. Brady Allred.

Thank you for your consideration.

In the above correspondence, I also add a brief bio. My biographical information and publications list are available on my Facebook page, but I also include my publications list when a publisher requests it in submission guidelines. Here's an example of one of the biographical paragraphs I use. They change over time, of course—I might add a recent premier, award, or other information that reveals my success and activity.

By way of introduction, I earned a bachelor of music degree in music education from the Eastman School of Music and a master of arts degree in teaching from Teachers College, Columbia University. I taught instrumental music in grades 4 through 12 in New York and in New Jersey. My concert band and string orchestra works have won contest awards and were selected in juried competitions for performances. My published works include music for concert band, choruses, string orchestra, and instrumental ensembles. I'm a member of the National Association for Music Education, the Florida Music Educators Association, and ASCAP.

8 Even though you've queried the publisher and gotten a submission go-ahead, blind submissions, like those described above, are one thing. Meeting publishers face to face, those who will evaluate your music for publication, is another thing, and the best course. Composer Michael J. Miller says, "Usually I send my music directly to the editor after building a rapport with that person. "I rarely submit via a generic submission link on a publisher's website. Building personal connections can go a long way in this regard. In addition, there is music that sells and there is music that doesn't. It is crucial to know what type of music a publisher is currently selling as well as what people are buying before submitting to a publisher. One can best learn these vital details by way of direct, personal contact with editors." For this reason, review the previous item #27.

When a publisher invites you to submit material in a face-to-face meeting, always include in your submission a reminder note on where and when you met. Also, check the publisher's website, and follow the submission guidelines to the letter—unless the publisher has asked for something different in person.

9 Some publishers acknowledge submissions; some don't. If you hear nothing on a submission in two months, email an inquiry about the work's submission status.

For example:

Dear Xxxxxxx: I'm emailing to learn the review status of [name of work], my [difficulty level] work for [instrumentation]. I had emailed [or mailed] the PDF score, mp3 playback file, and conductor notes on [date].

There's no hurry. I'm just seeking to become more familiar with your review process.

Waiting is the difficult part of submission. While you wait, keep researching publishers and honing your submissions list. Be ready with the next publisher when you receive a rejection. If you still receive no response, move on.

When I submit music to a publisher with whom I've not yet worked, I most often send only one piece. With a new publisher, I want to review the contract first, and if we agree on terms, I want to see how the process goes—how it is working with the publisher. If I'm submitting music to a publisher who already publishes my music, I might submit one, two, or three pieces.

Let serendipity work for you

Several years ago, I had submitted a wind quintet for publication consideration. I never heard from the publisher, so I assumed they weren't interested. Then, seven months later, I received an email from the publisher out of the blue, saying that if the piece were still available, they'd be glad to add it their catalog.

Music publishing can certainly seem capricious and unpredictable. The lesson here, then, is that it's important to get your music "out there" for publication consideration, to have many irons in the fire. Sure, you garner rejections, but sometimes, serendipity works in your favor. Getting your pieces into the marketplace, out for performance, and in various media for review gives serendipity a chance to work for you.

34 Enter contests and competitions.

I began entering my music in competitions only during the last few years, and I've been fortunate to have won some and been named a winner in others (with co-winners). The best, and, unfortunately, rarer, competitions are those that have no entry fee and that provide entrants with feedback. I do consider submitting music to contests that look promising with very modest entry fees.

Winning or placing in contests has been inspirational to me, it has boosted my confidence, and it's a resume enhancer. Learn who's running contests for the kind of music you write by periodically conducting Google searches on topics such as "orchestra composition competition" and similar phrases that include the genres or ensembles in which you compose and words like "competition" and "contest." Organizations and groups to which you belong and that you might consider joining may list or conduct competitions.

One main advantage to entering composing competitions is exposure. In many cases, the judges, or at least, some of them, include ensemble conductors and publishers. Putting your music in front of these people, whether you win or not, is beneficial. These judges may follow you on Facebook or on your website, they could contact you to perform your music, or they might recommend your music to other directors for performance.

Some years ago, I entered Imagine Music Publishing's composition contests, and I was fortunate to win several times. These wins led to publication of the winning pieces and several other submissions.

With placing and winning these contests, I gained more confidence in my work, and it inspired me with a flood of music ideas. However, I've had many more contest losses than wins, and this experience has also been valuable. Unfortunately, the way of the music composition world is that there is considerably more rejection than acceptance, so it's beneficial to learn how to accept rejection while maintaining your will to continue and to succeed. For more information in this area, see the next item.

Another view of contests and competitions appears here: https://nmbx.newmusicusa.org/dissing-the-competition/. This article, written by contributor composer Alex Shapiro, provides an insider's look into composing competitions, and I think it's a must read. For a wider perspective on standing out from the crowd and establishing a fulfilling composing career, read this article: https://nmbx.newmusicusa.org/lets-make-a-list/. The gist of this article, also written by Alex Shapiro, offers excellent suggestions how to take stock in one's professional goals and aspirations, and how to match these qualities with the vast world of opportunities for composers.

35 Prepare for rejection and use it to your advantage.

I once read that Margaret Mitchell's book *Gone with the Wind* was rejected 38 times before it was accepted for publication, and that Stephen King's *Carrie* was rejected 30 times before it was accepted for publication. You can find many, many more examples of great works that were rejected before they were published, so take heart: Rejections are as much a part of composing for publication as are acceptances.

It pays to insulate yourself against these frequent inevitabilities and learn how to benefit from them. Composers, those who endure, at least, receive plenty of rejections. In fact, count on them. There are many, many reasons why publishers reject work. Most of these reasons are business decisions. They are not personal. Your work is rejected. You are not. Keeping this fact foremost in mind is vital to maintaining your will to succeed and to keeping a professional demeanor.

Truth be told, when I receive a rejection, I pout and feel sorry for myself—briefly. I then read it carefully to find clues to a reason. Sometimes rejection letters are helpful with genuine criticism, and sometimes a rejection letter-writer will suggest another market for your work, or constructive ideas to improve its publishability with the company to which you've submitted the material. Consider these comments with a clear head and open mind. These kinds of comments can help you revise your work, if you deem that appropriate, or place your work in the right market.

For example, I had submitted a wind quintet for publication, but it was rejected. The rejection included a personal letter with the specific suggestion that the horn part was too difficult for the overall difficulty level of the piece. I reconsidered the piece and saw that the criticism was valid, so I rewrote some of the horn part and adjusted the other parts accordingly.

Sadly, you may never know the real reason(s) why a piece is rejected. That's why personal notes in rejection letters can be so valuable.

In addition, some rejection letters include an invitation to submit more material. That's great when that happens! These kinds of rejections are most often from publishers who acknowledge your skill and talent. Heed their advice and try again! These rejections are the coveted foot in the door if the person who sent the letter is an editor or the person who actually evaluates music for publication. If the person who sent you the rejection is the person who reviews the music, send the next submission directly to that person.

The business of accepting or rejecting music for publication can seem fickle. A few years ago, I submitted three concert band works to a publisher, two of which I thought were sure shots for acceptance and one that I thought was iffy but decided to send anyway. Guess which piece the publisher accepted? Right—the one that I thought had the least chance of acceptance! Prepare for this unpredictable ride. Here are just a few reasons why a publisher rejects music for publication:

- The piece is too long, or it's too short for the intended players.
- The instrument ranges are too difficult for a certain staff or staffs.
- The piece is too difficult, or it's too easy, or some parts are easier or more difficult.
- The work's harmony is too simple or too complex.
- The publisher's catalog already includes a similar work or similar works.
- The publisher's catalog has no similar works.
- The publisher has filled all the available publishing slots with works by its established composers.
- The publisher doesn't believe the piece will sell well.
- The submission timing is out of the publisher's "season" for reviewing material.
- The manuscript is illegible, or it would require too much time to clean up.
- The submission doesn't include a live performance (required by some publishers).
- The recording's performance or quality is unacceptable.

Use these criteria to evaluate a piece before you submit it. Make changes to completed works and compose new material accordingly.

You never want to submit a piece that's incomplete, poorly engraved, or poorly recorded. Still, I believe the lesson here is, when in doubt, submit.

Sometimes, publishers simply don't respond to a submission. Yup—that's a rejection, too, and it's the worst kind. See the previous item #33 to review how to handle a publisher's unresponsiveness.

36 Study the publishing contract.

Acceptances for publication are special times for me—joyous, exhilarating, and affirming, and, I admit, just as a rejection puts me momentarily in the dumps, an acceptance creates a very short moment of gloating. But even though acceptances are indeed wonderful, the devil is surely in the details of the publishing contract.

The contract you are offered is a legal document not to be taken lightly. Most publishers want the best for your work, for you, and for their investment in your product. Still, do not make assumptions about a publisher's intent. Publisher contracts often favor the publisher. They are often printed documents, which, by their appearance, discourage your amending them. If you can, it pays to have a lawyer read your contract to make sure it includes all, or most, of your expectations.

Several of my publishers have discussed contract terms with me before sending me a contract, so there was no need for my making changes. On the other hand, I've riddled some contracts with additions and changes. In these circumstances, it's best to call the publisher to negotiate. I've done that, too.

Sometimes it works; sometimes it doesn't. Remember that wind quintet I mentioned a few pages back? I made those changes to the horn part and resubmitted the work to another publisher, who accepted it for publication. However, I believed the contract was so unfair, I had practically rewritten it. When I returned the contract with my changes and signature, the publisher declined to agree to my changes, and, in fact, the publisher refused to renegotiate, so the deal fell through.

In retrospect, when I saw that I would require so many contract changes, I should have taken my own advice and phoned the publisher to bargain. When these disappointments occur, I remember this book's epigraph and the experiences of Margaret Mitchell, Stephen King, and many others.

Search online for sample music publishing contracts. These items can be useful guides to understanding contract terms and what is considered "standard." Although they would likely not provide legal assistance, some Facebook composer pages can direct you to examples of favorable music publishing terms and contracts.

In my experience, most publishers understand the needs of composers, and they work with new contributors and their "stable" of composers to make them happy and loyal.

"It's vital for any composer, no matter how well versed they think they may be in copyright and contract law, to ask a music attorney to review a contract before signing it," says composer Alex Shapiro. "This is a rule not only for publishing contracts, but for those addressing commissioning, licensing, synchronization, and mechanical rights as well. Additionally, contracts are essential for any collaboration/co-writing partnerships. Once a career gets up and running, these kinds of contracts will be coming down the pike quite regularly."

Shapiro continues, "I speak about copyright and contract terms all over the world on behalf of ASCAP, on whose board I sit. Yet almost every time I send my attorney a new contract I've received, he has something quite valuable and protective to add. I just can't stress getting legal representation enough."

37 Self-publish your music.

An alternative to submitting material for publication elsewhere is to self-publish your music. I have noticed more composers doing this in the past decades. The benefits are that you maintain complete copyright control over your music and you reap considerably more of the profits from sales and performance licenses—you'd register with licensing organizations as the writer and publisher, thus earning the full 100% of those royalties.

"A composer colleague advised me to self-publish and to join a PRO (performance rights organization) as both a writer and a publisher to be able to earn double the royalties," says composer Rain Worthington. "Uploading scores to the digital distribution sites, such as Sheet Music Plus, is another venue for generating income. This is especially true for composers of choral music, and those composers who are involved in creating arrangements of songs. Joining and uploading scores to these digital sheet music sales sites is usually a simple process, and in my experience, the sites seem to be legitimate in their revenue reporting and financial contracts with composer/publishers."

Composer Elizabeth Raum says, "When you self-publish, you keep the copyright, although many publishers these days allow you to do that. In the old days when they had to engrave your music at great expense and then market it (before the days of the internet), publishers needed compensation, but these days you probably don't need a publisher if you don't mind trying to keep track of payments and know how to send PDFs that can only be copied once. I think most of my music is publicized by word of mouth and YouTube."

Composer Raymond Burkhart has been self-publishing his music for a long time. "I could see, from the very emergence of desktop computers and music notation software, that self-publishing would be big," he says. "It's been big for some time now, and I think it will only get bigger, as technology eases the delivery of print products. We've all seen how self-publishing and the internet have democratized all publishing. I also didn't want to give up my copyrights to a publisher that might decide at some point no longer to make my pieces available.

"There is surely a tradeoff in making this decision, a worthy topic that I cannot really address here, but I found it a huge attraction to start self-publishing and see where that would lead. I'd say that some music self-publishers have found more sales success than I, and many have had less. But really, it's not a competition or race—at least, not for me. I took on this work to sustain the availability of my works to the public and to take on a project that I'd never considered until my 20s. It's worth noting that I recently team-taught a composition course with two composers just a decade or so older than I am, well known composers with composer friends of the generation before the phenomenon of self-publishing, and one fielded the question,

'How best can I get published?', by saying, 'Great question. With the possibility now of self-publishing, all my friends are trying to get out of their publishing contracts!'"

The disadvantages of self-publishing are that you must promote your own music, print it, and manage a complete publishing business, which takes time away from composing. Setting up and running a business incurs extra expenses, too, including accounting, permits, and taxes, depending on where you live, all taking time away from composing.

38 Be thoroughly professional in your dealings with everyone.

I consider some conduct to be hallmarks of "professional" behavior. I've adopted them and so should you:

- Don't burn bridges. I've known people who severed relationships with colleagues unnecessarily. Sometimes ending a bad professional alliance is appropriate, surely, but such dire action is often neither wise nor fitting. For this reason, when I'm insulted, angry, or hurt and tempted to take immediate action, I muster all my restraint and wait a day or two before taking any action. In these circumstances, after a cooling-off period, the actions I've taken were usually different from my initial inclinations, and I'm glad and relieved that I didn't respond rashly.

I wait this way because you never know where someone has just been, the news that person may have just received, or that person's circumstances. Consider this: When my daughter was in high school, she worked the counter at a local pharmacy. At first, she'd come home in tears, complaining how customers treated her. Then one day she said, "Bad treatment gets to me a lot less, now that I understand you never know a customer's situation—the guy picking up a prescription who has just received devastating news from his doctor, or the woman who's been in constant, increasing pain for months. Some people are just plain nasty, but most people deserve compassion, understanding, and forgiveness."

Remembering my daughter's advice, I try my best to be patient with colleagues and give everyone the benefit of the doubt. For this reason, after considering dire action, I often just don't respond, or I answer with far more kindness, understanding, and tact than I had initially considered.

- Write down all your insights, ideas, and reminders. Use your smart phone notes, voice memos, reminders, and calendar features for this purpose. Don't rely on your memory, even if your recall is tack-sharp. Be a model of organization.
- Learn how to work with people. All the technical skills a composer could have don't amount to much without the ability to work with colleagues and associates—and that means learning to get the job done with people you dislike, people who don't like you, difficult people, back-stabbers, complainers—all kinds of people, easy to work with and hard to work with. No matter what your professional aspirations are, invest in learning to work with all kinds of collaborators.

Working with these kinds of people is no easy task. The behaviors that have worked for me include:

* Making things cordial but strictly business—impersonal. Stick to the tasks at hand. And when you disagree, it's not, "I disagree

with you." It's "I disagree with that idea." The latter has a far less insulting ring to it—it's not about the person. It's about the idea.

* Be assertive. Assertive behavior is not aggression. In assertive behavior, you use a lot of "I" sentences. I prefer this, I suggest that, I think this. People often hear "you" language as insulting, degrading, and accusing.
* Watch your tone. Never shout. Be objective and businesslike, but be sincere.
* Don't dawdle. Get the job done and leave.
* Don't gossip, and don't contribute to gossip.

- Mind your manners. Much of my work these days is done online—not in person. Nevertheless, on the phone, in emails and letters, and in person: Watch your language—keep it clean, even when your correspondent doesn't. Don't use language that could offend someone. Say nothing demeaning. Avoid politics and locker room talk. If someone tries to goad you into these kinds of discussions, walk away or remain silent. Stay positive and focused on the task at hand.
- Never, ever, under any circumstances miss a deadline. When I began writing my first regular magazine column for *Pennsylvania Angler & Boater* magazine (I've always loved fishing and writing about it), former editor the late Jim Yoder set me straight on how we were going to work together. "If you think I'm a dictator," he said, "you're right. Never, ever miss a deadline with me. Never. If you miss one, sure, there might be a reasonable explanation, but NEVER an excuse. Just don't miss 'em."

- I know the crucial importance of this maxim as an editor, writer, and composer. Your professional reputation hinges at least in part on meeting all deadlines.
- Under-promise and over-deliver. Don't promise more than you can deliver and then be forced to disappoint someone. For instance, when you need to establish a submission deadline for your material, give yourself PLENTY of time and then make sure you beat, not just meet, your own deadline by delivering the goods early.
- Always arrive early for appointments, meetings, and scheduled events. Legendary Green Bay Packers football coach Vince Lombardi is said to have set his watch 10 or 15 minutes ahead so that he and his team were never late for meetings. To this day, this is known as "Lombardi time."
- Similarly, be prepared with necessary and appropriate items for all appointments, meetings, and scheduled events.
- Follow through on promises. If you say you'll get back to someone at a certain time, do so. If you say you'll return a phone call, do it. If you say you'll meet someone at a certain time and place, do it. Deliver what you say you'll deliver and when you say you'll deliver it—every time.

Following through on promises means staying organized with your calendar and contacts. There are many calendar and contact app substitutes for apps that you might already have on your computer or smartphone. I have found these alternative apps unnecessary. The inherent calendar and reminder apps on my iPhone sync via iCloud with the Mac OS X apps on my MacBook Air and iMac, and this arrangement has been productive and easy for me.

- Be honest with everyone. When you make a mistake in working with others, admit it, apologize, fix it, and move on—quickly. When others make mistakes, fix the problem if you can and move on with the project without blaming anyone and without dwelling on the error. I used to work with someone who put it this way: "When the ball goes out of bounds, my job is to get it back in play quickly. I don't care who tossed it out of bounds. I get the ball back in play fast and move on." Exactly!

39 Seek commissions.

A commissioned work has already received an initial critical review by the commissioning party. So even though many, many factors affect acceptance for publication, commissioned works have an advantage over non-commissioned works.

Composer Raymond Burkhart says, "Money, of course, is another reason to seek commissions, since money helps pay the bills while we write more music. Ever greater notoriety helps get more commissions and better fees, which in turn help pay more bills and enable you to write more music."

There is a higher purpose to seeking commission. "A composer may leave for future generations music of great value, value measured no longer in dollars and of no use to the composer, but which might entertain, uplift, and inspire the human race long after a composer's physical departure," says Burkhart.

40 Check resources often because they change.

Useful reference books, websites, hardware, software, and new opportunities are always appearing and changing. Be aware of new resources, but remember that what's new isn't necessarily better. For this reason, evaluate what's "new" by scrutinizing reviews, reading online forums, and getting recommendations. Do not buy on impulse.

41 Practice, practice, practice.

You know the old joke: A neatly dressed man with a violin case asks a vagrant in New York City, "How do I get to Carnegie Hall?" The vagrant thinks for a second and says, "Practice. Practice. Practice." This old witticism still rings true.

For composers, this "practice" idea means regularly practicing one's instrument(s) and craft, and regularly applying the ideas in this book. This suggestion is also a practical application of this book's epigraph.

42 Take a wider view.

This book reveals the path that I have taken in my composing. So it's vital to say that these career choices are certainly not the only ones that lead to a successful composing career. My choices were right for me. Thus, I have delineated the steps I take in traditional publishing. Truth is, based on what I've learned in writing this book, I may self-publish my work in the future.

Nevertheless, does it surprise you that many successful, widely performed composers have never won many composing contest awards and have never routinely submitted music to traditional publishers? Finding your own path in this bewildering maze can be difficult what with all the choices available. Staying on the right path for you requires constant evaluation of your heart's desires, your personal and monetary goals, blending and balancing these elements, and embracing widely accepted professional standards and practices (refer to item #38, "Be thoroughly professional in your dealings with everyone").

To find one's way, keep two ideas in mind: 1) understand that most composers do not make a living solely from composing, and 2) being published in a traditional way doesn't always mean that your music is widely performed.

To illustrate these ideas, consider my experience. With a bachelor's degree and a master's degree in teaching music, I initially taught public school instrumental music while composing. I also contributed articles and photographs first to state music teacher association magazines and then to national music teaching publications. Writing words led to my changing careers from teaching to writing and editing—I became an associate editor of *The Instrumentalist* magazine for a year, then for another year managing editor of *Music Educators Journal*, and then for some 26 years, editor of *Pennsylvania Angler & Boater* magazine (I've always been a passionate angler and boater).

The point is that during these career changes, I continued to compose. My networking in these pursuits, the music ones, at least, enriched my composing skills, increased my productivity, and helped me get my music performed.

Other widely performed composers include music preparation pros, conductors, arrangers, music editors, recording engineers, recording studio assistants, and music librarians. The list of supplemental employment among composers is considerably larger than just those I have mentioned. In this book's Resources section, read the contributor bios carefully to discover their angles on how they achieve success. You'll find a wealth of encouragement and ideas there that you can harness.

43 Trust the processes of learning these skills, of becoming increasingly more adept at composing, of becoming more prolific, and of promoting your work.

Be patient and persistent. Manage your time. Keep learning and becoming more skilled. Stay focused on your goals. Learn to please yourself. If you genuinely enjoy your work and please yourself, you will ultimately please audiences. Review this book's epigraph, and persevere!

Author's Note

Thank you for purchasing and reading my book. I hope you found it useful. If you did, please leave a review on the website where you bought the book. Thanks again.

– Art Michaels

Resources

A. General Creativity Books

The Artist's Way
by Julia Cameron

Breakthrough!: Proven Strategies to Overcome Creative Block and Spark Your Imagination
by Alex Cornell

The Creative Habit: Learn It and Use It for Life
by Twyla Tharp with Mark Reiter

Creativity, Inc.: Overcoming the Unseen Forces That Stand in the Way of True Inspiration
by Ed Catmull, Amy Wallace

Focus: The Hidden Driver of Excellence
by Daniel Goleman

Maximize your potential: grow your expertise, take bold risks & build an incredible career
by Jocelyn K. Glei

On Knowing: Essays for the Left Hand, Second Edition
by Jerome Bruner

A Technique for Producing Ideas: The simple, five-step formula anyone can use to be more creative in business and in life!
by James Webb Young

Uncommon Genius: How Great Ideas are Born
by Denise Shekerjian

V Is for Vulnerable: Life Outside the Comfort Zone
by Seth Godin

The War of Art
by Steven Pressfield

Werner Herzog: A Guide for the Perplexed: Conversations with Paul Cronin
by Paul Cronin

B. General Creativity Websites

http://www.businessballs.com/business-networking.htm

http://99u.com/

http://www.creativeboom.com/resources/100-of-the-freshest-blogs-and-websites-for-creative-entrepreneurs-in-2016/

C. Video Calling

FaceTime—http://www.apple.com/mac/facetime

Google Hangouts—https://hangouts.google.com

GoTo Meeting—http://www.gotomeeting.com

Skype—www.skype.com

UberConference—https://www.uberconference.com

Zoom—https://zoom.us

D. Composing

1. General Reference Books

The Complete Rhyming Dictionary: Including The Poet's Craft Book Revised Edition
by Clement Wood

The Inner Game of Music
by Barry Green

Music Composition: Craft and Art
by Alan Belkin

Songwriters on Songwriting
by Paul Zollo

2. Music Theory Books

Basic Music Theory, 4th ed.: How to Read, Write, and Understand Written Music
by Jonathan Harnum

Alfred's Essentials of Music Theory: A Complete Self-Study Course for All Musicians
by Andrew Surmani

Harmony Fifth Edition
by Walter Piston

Materials and Techniques of Twentieth Century Music
by Stefan Kostka

Twentieth Century Harmony
by Vincent Persichetti

Helpful New Ideas for The Understanding Of 18th Century Harmony
by W. Francis McBeth

Graduate Music Theory Review
(in Outline Form)
by James R. Riley

3. Music History Books

Concise History of Western Music (Fifth Edition)
by Barbara Russano Hanning

Game Sound
by Karen Collins

The History of Jazz
by Ted Gioia

Showtime: A History of the Broadway Musical Theater
by Larry Stempel

The Vintage Guide to Classical Music
by Jan Swafford

4. Orchestration Books

Arranging for the Concert Band
by Frank Erickson

Band Scoring
by Joseph Wagner

The Cambridge Guide to Orchestration
by Ertuğrul Sevsay

Handbook of Instrumentation
by Andrew Stiller

Instrumentation and Orchestration
by Alfred Blatter

Orchestration
by Cecil Forsyth

Orchestration
by Walter Piston

Orchestration: A Practical Handbook
by Joseph Wagner

Principles of Orchestration
by Nikolay Rimsky-Korsakov

The Study of Orchestration
by Samuel Adler

Techniques of Orchestration
by Kent Kennan

5. Music Notation Reference Books

Behind Bars: The Definitive Guide to Music Notation
by Elaine Gould

Music Notation in the Twentieth Century: A Practical Guidebook
by Kurt Stone

Music Notation: A Manual of Modern Practice
by Gardner Read

6. General Music Reference Books

The Harvard Dictionary of Music
edited by Don Michael Randel

7. Music Business Books

All You Need to Know About the Music Business: 10th Edition
by Donald S. Passman

Music Money and Success 8th Edition: The Insider's Guide to Making Money in the Music Business
by Jeff Brabec and Todd Brabec

What They'll Never Tell You About the Music Business, Third Edition: The Complete Guide for Musicians, Songwriters, Producers, Managers, Industry Executives, Attorneys, Investors, and Accountants
by Peter M. Thall

8. Composing Websites

a. Online Composer Forums, Blogs, eZines

www.composeforums.com

https://composersforum.org

http://notat.io

Facebook: Tonal Composers Group

Facebook: Composers Group

Facebook: 21st Century Classical Music Group

Facebook: Orchestration Online Group

Facebook: Is This Playable? Group

New Music Box—https://nmbx.newmusicusa.org

b. Music Notation Products

Crescendo (http://www.nch.com.au/notation/)

Dorico—http://www.steinberg.net/en/products/dorico/start.html

Finale and its product family—www.makemusic.com

LilyPond—http://www.lilypond.org/

MuseScore—https://musescore.org/

Music Studio—https://itunes.apple.com/us/app/music-studio/id328608539?mt=8&ign-mpt=uo%3D4 (iPad, iPhone, iPod Touch app)

NotateMe Now—https://itunes.apple.com/au/app/notateme-now/id783567215?mt=8 (iPhone and iPad app)

Noteflight—https://www.noteflight.com/login (iPad app)

Notion—http://www.presonus.com/products/Notion-for-iOS (iPad app)

Sibelius—www.sibelius.com

StaffPad—https://www.staffpad.net (Windows and iPad)

Symphony Pro 4—https://itunes.apple.com/us/app/symphony-pro-4/id412380315?mt=8&ign-mpt=uo%3D4 (iPad app)

c. Music Readers

forScore (for ipad, iphone, and iPod Touch)—https://forscore.co

MobileSheets—https://www.zubersoft.com/mobilesheets/ (Windows, Android)

MusicReader—https://www.musicreader.net (Windows)

d. DAWs (digital audio workstation)

Cubase—http://www.steinberg.net/en/products/cubase/start.html

Digital Performer—https://motu.com/products/software/dp/

GarageBand—http://www.apple.com/ios/garageband/Reason (for iPad, iPhone, and iPod touch)

Logic Pro—https://www.apple.com/logic-pro/

Presonus Studio One—https://www.presonus.com/products/Studio-One

Pro Tools—http://www.avid.com/us/products/family/pro-tools

Reaper—http://www.reaper.fm/

Sonar—https://www.cakewalk.com/products/SONAR/

StudioOne—http://studioone.presonus.com/

e. Sample Libraries

East West—www.soundsonline.com

Garritan Virtual Instrument Libraries (Personal Orchestra 5)—www.garritan.com

Heavyocity—www.heavyocity.com

Native Instruments—www.native-instruments.com

NotePerformer—www.noteperformer.com

Output—www.output.com/products

Spitfire Audio—www.spitfireaudio.com

Spectrasonics—www.spectrasonics.net

Synthogy—https://synthogy.com

Vienna Symphonic Library—www.vsl.co.at/en/Software/Vienna_Ensemble/

f. Miscellaneous Music Websites

Abebooks.com—used and out-of-print books at great prices

Free staff paper to print—www.teoria.com

IMSLP Petrucci Library—imslp.org/wiki/Main_Page

Instrumental Studies for Eyes and Ears—resources.music.indiana.edu/isfee/

Music theory website—www.teoria.com

E. Composer Advocacy Organizations

American Composers Forum—https://composersforum.org

Chamber Music America—www.chamber-music.org

NewMusicUSA—www.newmusicusa.org

Society of Composers & Lyricists—https://thescl.com

Contributors

1. The Author

Arthur J. Michaels is an award-winning composer, trained formally as a music educator. He earned a bachelor of music degree in music education from the Eastman School of Music and a master of arts degree in teaching from Teachers College, Columbia University. He taught instrumental music in grades 4 through 12 for nine years. Since 1978, he's published music for concert band, string orchestra, instrumental ensembles, and choruses.

He is also a seasoned, award-winning writer, editor, and photographer. He was chief of Educational Media for the Pennsylvania Fish & Boat Commission and for 26 year he was editor of *Pennsylvania Angler & Boater* magazines. He was an associate editor of *The Instrumentalist* magazine and managing editor of *Music Educators Journal*. He's contributed chapters and photographs to several books. He also co-authored and photographed *Starting in Taekwondo* and *Kickboxing Basics*, both of which were published by Sterling Publishing Co., Inc. He also wrote and photographed *Pennsylvania Overlooks*, published by Penn State Press. He's been a freelance writer and photographer since 1973, having published more than 600 articles and many more photographs.

2. Contributor Bios

Ronald J. Brown

Ronald J. Brown studied violin and flamenco guitar as an adolescent. After a BA from Concordia University in Montreal, he received his Diploma in Education from McGill University. He has worked as a high school English teacher, a computer programmer and analyst, income tax specialist, and B&B owner. In his mid-50s he attended Carleton University in Ottawa, studying contemporary music theory. He also studied with Dr. Alan Belkin of the Université de Montréal. He is a founding member of http://www.composeforums.com, a discussion group for established and new composers and has had works performed in Japan; France; Seattle, Washington; and Montreal, Quebec.

Raymond David Burkhart, PhD

Raymond David Burkhart, PhD, earned music degrees from Occidental College, the University of Southern California, and Claremont Graduate University. He is recognized for his achievements as a composer, trumpeter, musicologist, educator, and conductor. He is listed in *Trumpet Greats: A Biographical Dictionary* and has over 100 works in publication. He has conducted professional, community, and youth orchestras, concert bands, jazz ensembles, chamber opera, and musical theater. He has given papers in New York, Paris, Edinburgh, and Glasgow and taught at Pomona College, Glendale College, Pasadena City College, and Occidental College. He has also worked as an expert witness and forensic musicologist. He is a member of ASCAP, the American Federation of Musicians, the Historic Brass Society, and Pi Kappa Lambda.

Christopher Carlone

Christopher Carlone is a composer and sound designer from western Connecticut. He holds two degrees in music from the University of New Hampshire and the University of Massachusetts. Carlone is known mostly for his scoring on popular YouTube channels such as Comics and Riot Games' Animated Cartoons. Christopher's background music has been viewed over 200 million times on popular YouTube animations. He is currently on the faculty as the instrumental music director at the Sherman School and continues to compose for series featured on Amazon Prime and Hulu.

Laurie Jeanne Crockett

Laurie Jeanne Crockett received her bachelor's degree in English education and a masters of science degree in remedial reading. She has studied piano for 13 years. She began composing piano instrumentals in 2012 and transitioned to sacred vocal works including Christmas and Easter cantatas performed in local churches. During her time as librarian at the Jordanville (NY) public library, she was awarded the Individual Artist Grant by the Central New York Arts Council to produce two musicals performed for the summer reading program with the cast comprised of the local community. She has also produced a Christmas CD for piano and voice, and a piano instrumental CD, "A Simple Life." She is a regular contributor to Pond5 and a member of ASCAP.

Kim Diehnelt

Trained in the United States and Europe, Kim Diehnelt established her craft as a conductor and composer in Finland and Switzerland. She has been composing works for solo instruments, chamber groups, and orchestral and choral ensembles since 2011. Her style is best described as a "Nordic Palestrina," as her works possess a lyrical, vocal quality with an attention to beauty and the sense of an unfolding story. She was a semi-finalist for The American Prize in Composition in the Professional Orchestra division in 2015 for her work "Montegar" for viola and strings. An active guest conductor in the United States and abroad, she is acknowledged as an authority on the music of Edward Elgar. Kim was named the KISMET Foundation's 2018 Artist-in-Residence.

Paolo Fradiani

Paolo Fradiani earned a master's degree with honors in composition and jazz. He studied at the State Conservatory of

Music Alfredo Casella in L'Aquila, Italy and at the Hochschule für Musik in Mannheim, Germany. His works have been performed in Europe and North America by orchestras, ensembles, and soloists including the Berliner Philharmoniker soloists. He has received several prizes by the Italian Ministry of Education and the Italian Ministry of Cultural Heritage and Activities and Tourism. He has also been composer in residence at Società Aquilana dei Concerti "B. Barattelli." He is founder and artistic director of the Orchestra da Camera della Marsica. His works are published by Da Vinci Edition, Donemus Publishing, Edition Margaux, and Universal Edition.

Divan Gattamorta

Brazilian composer, musician, and multi-instrumentalist Divan Gattamorta creates music for the dance. Since 1985 he has worked at the State University of Campinas/Brazil, playing in modern dance classes, and in contemporary and Brasil dances. He is a graduate in saxophone and pedagogy from the Ulbra and did post-graduate studies in soundtracks for cinema and TV at the University Anhembi-Morumbi in São Paulo. He has worked on over 40 original soundtracks and several albums for contemporary and modern dance classes. His music is played worldwide in classrooms and in theatrical dance performances.

Mike Hall

Mike Hall has over 25 years experience in sound design, composing, producing, engineering, and mastering music for a vast variety of musical styles. He has worked in many forms of media that include audio cds/vinyl, film/video, and gaming for projects all over the world. "I have a huge passion in what I do involving the creation of music for myself and for others," he says. "I shall continue this passion working with others worldwide to help develop the best artistic visions of sound."

R. Duane Hendricks

R. Duane Hendricks is a composer, conductor, trombonist, pianist, artist, and teacher. He composes for wind and brass ensembles, classical guitar, and trombones. He conducts the Rocky Mountain Concert Band in Calgary and guest conducts other ensembles. As a trombonist he has played in orchestras, recordings, and concert, brass, circus and dance bands. As a pianist he has played with instrumental and vocal soloists, and for opera rehearsals and choirs. As an artist he works mainly in dry pastel and enjoys landscape painting. As a teacher he taught music in schools for several decades, and continues to teach trombone, piano, guitar and composition in his studio, working with students of all ages who love to make music and discover their talent.

Zander Hulme

Zander Hulme is an Australian composer and sound designer, and founder of the game audio company Supertonic. He specializes in interactive music systems and technical sound design for indie games, striving to immerse players in dynamic game worlds. Zander has given talks on his process at universities and industry conferences, including Games Connect Asia Pacific. He also helps run Game Audio Brisbane, a local community group for aspiring game sound professionals. His work in animated films has won awards and has been screened at renowned international festivals such as Festival de Cannes and Bristol Encounters Short Film Festival.

Pamela Illanes -Tatsuoka

Pamela Illanes -Tatsuoka is a Chilean/American composer. She studied composition at Westminster College, NJ, Cuyahoga Community College, and the Cleveland Institute of Music. Her music has been performed by various ensembles including the Orquesta Sinfonica Juvenil Rocas de Santo Domingo Chile, the Orquesta Sinfonica Municipal Copiapo, the Conservatorio Profesional de Musica de Guadalajara, Spain, and the University of San Francisco. She has collaborated with Chilean writer Antonio Skarmeta, setting his poems to music. This collaboration was featured in a documentary about Antonio that aired on the Television Nacional de Chile. Pamela also has written songs based on Pablo Neruda poems that have been approved by the Pablo Neruda Foundation. She has produced several books and CDs, and she has collaborated with visual artists to develop interactive art exhibitions based on her music.

Grahame Gordon Innes

Grahame Gordon Innes was largely self-taught, having studied music only for three years at the end of secondary school from age 15 to 18. He completed his studies of music theory and composition on his own, announcing his arrival as a composer with Symphony No. 1, "Nordic," in 1989. He has worked as a teacher of violin, viola, cello, piano, music theory, and composition since 1988, eventually being sought out for private tuition by graduate and post-graduate students struggling with assignments, and for advice from composers starting out in their career. To date he has written 23 symphonies and eight concertos, a string serenade, a tone poem, and a few compositions for chamber orchestra. He contributes regularly to Quora and is active on Facebook and Youtube.

Glenn Martin

Glenn Martin, composer, arranger, and jazz trombonist, earned a bachelor of science degree in music education from Tennessee Technological University and a master of music degree in music theory-composition from the University of Louisiana. He also did post-graduate work at the University of Georgia and the University of North Texas. His works have been published by CPP/Belwin-Warner Brothers (Alfred Music), R.B.C. Music, the International Tuba Euphonium Association Press, and Cimarron Music Press. He taught high school instrumental music for 12 years, directing superior-rated concert, marching, and jazz bands. He taught trombone, music theory, jazz band, and music technology courses at Cumberland University and privately. At Tennessee State University, he taught music theory courses, music history, and jazz combo, and at the University of North Texas, he taught jazz improvisation.

Michael J. Miller

Michael J. Miller is a freelance composer. He has a master's degree in conducting from the University of Florida and a bachelor's degree in music education from Syracuse University. His music is published by Alfred, F.J.H., Carl Fischer, Eighth Note Publications, and most recently composer Larry Clark's Excelcia Music. Michael's music is in high demand, having been named to Band World's best 100 new works for band, J.W. Pepper's Editor's choice, and performed at the Midwest Band and Orchestra Clinic. Michael also designs for marching bands across the United States. He is the brass arranger for the Colts Drum and Bugle Corps (Dubuque, Iowa). His music for marching band has been performed at the Superbowl and several B.C.S. (Bowl Championship Series) bowl games. To learn more about Michael and his music, visit www.michaeljmillermusic.com.

Teresa O'Connell

Teresa O'Connell is the owner of TJO Music and Consulting. A BMI composer/arranger, professional pianist/accompanist, and private educator (voice, piano, and English/Language Arts), Teresa has over 30 years experience as an award-winning choral director/music teacher and English/language public school educator in grades K-college. Teresa also enjoys working in musical theatre as a director and musical director. Teresa loves teaching the very young to young at heart seniors. A lifelong church musician, Teresa has served in several churches as director of music, choir director, and pianist.

All of these experiences have led Teresa to composing for school music classes, ensembles, soloists, and church choirs. Her upbeat and positive-message songs are created to inspire singers and audiences alike.

Laura Pettigrew

Laura Pettigrew earned a bachelor of music degree in composition and flute performance and a master of music degree in composition from The University of Regina (Canada). Her works include orchestral, solo, chamber ensemble, choral, and concert band music. She has received world premieres, commissions from the Toronto Symphony Orchestra (Canada), and Grammy® Award–winning I Solisti Veneti (Italy), among others. Her works are featured on recordings by national and international soloists and ensembles. She has been the beneficiary of many scholarships and grants, including those from the Canada Council for the Arts, Saskatchewan Arts Board, Creative Saskatchewan, Saskatchewan Foundation for the Arts, Artist Award, Canadian Music Centre, Saskatchewan Film Tax Credit, and FACTOR. She is a member of the Canadian Music Center and SOCAN.

Elizabeth Raum

Canadian composer Elizabeth Raum began her musical career as an oboist and only turned her attention to composition at the age of 35 when she wrote her first opera, "The Final Bid," for four singers and chamber orchestra. This was followed by three other operas, two of which she wrote the librettos; concertos for violin, French horn, oboe, clarinet, trombone, euphonium, double bass, and tuba; several ballets including the music for a major ballet for the Royal Winnipeg Ballet; multi-media creations; music for chorus; major orchestral and band works; and a body of over 70 chamber pieces. She has also composed for film, having won several awards for her writing in this genre.

Ari Romppanen

Finnish composer Ari Romppanen holds a masters degree in music with a focus on composition from Sibelius-Academy in Helsinki, and bachelor of music in music education. He has also familiarized himself with theater dramaturgy and other performing arts, which has influenced his expression and formal works. Trained as a pianist, his music consists mainly of piano and chamber pieces, and several pianists from Finland, central Europe, and all the way from Japan have commissioned his works. He also performs as a pianist and he has worked as a piano and composition teacher. He has also won awards in both piano and composition contests.

Alex Shapiro

Alex Shapiro composes acoustic and electroacoustic pieces known for their lyricism and drama. Published by Activist Music LLC, her works are heard daily in concerts and broadcasts across the U.S. and internationally, and they can be found on 30 commercially released recordings from around the world. Alex is the Symphonic & Concert writer member on the Board of Directors of ASCAP, and also serves on the boards of The ASCAP Foundation and the The Aaron Copland Fund for Music. Alex lives on Washington State's remote San Juan Island, and when not composing she can be found communing with the sea life, as seen on her music and photo-filled website, www.alexshapiro.org.

Mark Taylor

Composer/bandleader Mark Taylor has been commissioned to compose for theatre, dance, and the concert stage. One of the few performers to successfully integrate the notoriously difficult French horn into the landscape of jazz and improvised music, Taylor's broad musical background includes performing, composing, and arranging. In addition to leading his own ensembles and releasing four CDs of all original material, he has also performed and recorded with an array of modern jazz giants including Max Roach, Henry Threadgill, Muhal Richard Abrams, and Anthony Braxton. His works include music for symphony orchestra, chamber ensembles, jazz ensembles, film, TV, and animation. Mark is a member of the Society of Composers and Lyricists and ASCAP.

Tony Tester

Tony Tester, has worked for many years as a freelance jingle writer in the U.K. and Scandinavia. At present, he is CEO of Melody Treehouse, a company that supplies educational songs and resources for teachers and parents of young children aged between 3 to 7 years. His two children's musicals "Cydara" & "Jenny and the Strange and Peculiar Land" were broadcast on 27 independent radio stations throughout the U.K. and were well received. Tony has also written the soundtracks and incidental music for a number of Norwegian short films, "Death May Die" and "Between the Roots & the Sea" and the video game "Gespalten." In 2015 he gained a First Class Honours Degree in Popular Music from the University of South Wales. Tony is a member of TONO (Norway) & PRS (United Kingdom).

Jukka Viitasaari

Jukka Viitasaari comes from the Finnish Ostrobothnian village of Kuortane, the birthplace of several other important Finnish musical and cultural figures. Originally trained as a teacher, Viitasaari has had many decades of success as a composer for wind bands, including many clever and successful pieces for elementary-level groups. He has been awarded seven Finnish and 13 international band composition contest prizes to date. He has more than sixty works published in Finland and several others in the U.S. He is the executive director of FinnBand-Finnish Band Publishers United, a board member of the Finnish Wind Band Association, a representative on the Finnish Music Council, and a member of the Society of Finnish Composers and Finnish Music Creators.

Sahlia Wong

Sahlia Wong is a composer for video games and film. Hailing from southwestern Ontario, Canada, her works have been recorded by the Budapest Art Orchestra and played by the St. Lawrence String Quartet, Windsor Symphony Orchestra String Quartet, the Kindred Spirits String Orchestra, University of Toronto Master Chorale, Boomwhacker Orchestra, and Windsor Centre for the Creative Arts Choir. Her song "Le Léon" received an award for Best Theme from the SOCAN Foundation Awards for Audio Visual Composers. A graduate of Berklee College of Music's Master of Music in Scoring for Film, Television, and Video Games, she also holds a Bachelor of Music in Composition degree from the University of Toronto, and an ARCT Diploma in Piano Performance from the Royal Conservatory of Music.

Rain Worthington

Rain Worthington's compositions have been performed from Brazil to Iceland, Japan to India. Self-taught in composition, her catalog includes works for orchestra, chamber ensembles, duos, solos and miniatures. Her orchestral compositions have been premiered in the U.S. and internationally with performances in Italy and Brazil. She has received the American Prize-Ernst Bacon Award, a Global Music award and grants from Meet The Composer, ASCAP, American Music Center, New York Foundation for the Arts, and American Composers Forum. Since 2016 she has served as Artistic Administrator/Composer Advocate for the New York Women Composers. Her music is recorded on PARMA Recordings/Navona Records.

Index

A

A Arte de Compor Música para o Cinema, 127

Aamano Music, 31

Actual Tonal Composers (Facebook group), 58

"Agnus Dei," 31-32

Alan Belkin, 99, 187, 196

Alesis Quadrasynth, 169

Alry Publications, 67, 72, 141

Amazon Drive, 76

Archetypi, 27

Arranging Music for the Real World, 126

Arranjo, 127

ASCAP, 130, 131, 158, 169, 197, 198, 205, 206, 208

Audacity, 109, 147

B

Backblaze, 76

Beethoven, 47, 48, 49

Behind Bars: The Definitive Guide to Music Notation, 125, 190

Bell Music Publishing, 71, 141

"Bluesy Chalumeau Cha-Cha," 34, 72, 85, 141

Bock/Harnick, 48

Borodin, 47

Brahms, 47, 48

"Brassy Capriccio," 72, 157

C

Canva.com, 148

Carrie, 163

Charlemagne Palestine, 67

Choralife.com, 32

Classical Archives-MIDI, 103

Composers (Facebook group), 58, 191

Conductors on Composing for Band, 125

"Copycat's Convoy," 141

D

"Dance Suite," 72

David Young, 111

"Days of Wine and Roses," 47

DAW (digital audio workstation), 23, 70, 107, 109, 116, 192

Delian Society, 131

Dorico, 107, 191

Dr. Darrell Scott, 48

Dropbox, 76, 78, 109

E

Eastman School of Music, 11, 12, 47, 48, 66, 104, 157, 158, 195

"Escapade in Swing", 85

Essentials of Music Theory: Complete, 126, 187

"Euphotrombotonia," 34, 71, 141

"Evening Prayer," 48

Everett Gates, 12, 66

F

Facebook, 58, 69, 79, 100, 117, 118, 121, 122, 128, 134, 135, 138-142, 144, 145, 149, 158, 162, 168, 191, 202

Finale, 21-23, 30-32, 34, 40, 74-76, 103, 105, 107-109, 111, 114, 147, 157-158, 191

"Fiorello!," 48

Findings, 127

Florida Music Educators Association, 131, 158

G

Glyph Studio S4000, 76

Gone with the Wind, 163

Google Calendar, 78

Google Drive, 76

Gusthold Music Publisher, 72

H

Handel, 48

"Hansel and Gretel," 48

Harmonia, 127

Harmonia Funcional, 127

Hearing and Writing Music, 126

Henry Threadgill, 68, 206

Hindemith, 47

Holysheetmusic.com, 32

Howard Hanson, 49

Hubspot, 79

Humperdinck, 48

I

iCloud, 76, 176

iDrive, 76

Imagine Music Publishers, 85, 162
iMovie, 146, 148-149
IMSLP Petrucci Music Library, 102, 194
iPhone, 21-22, 24, 30-31, 42-43, 79, 103, 136-137, 176, 191-192

J
"Jazzy Capriccio," 34, 85
Jim Yoder, 175

K
Komplete Kontrol S61, 28
"Kyrie," 48, 141

L
Lennon-McCartney, 46
Leonard Bernstein, 47, 127
"Lida Rose," 48
LilyPond, 107, 191
LinkedIn, 69, 79, 121, 134-135, 138-140, 149
"Little Concert Overture with Fanfare," 142
Lou Bynum, 12, 66

M
MacBook Air, 76, 108, 176
Mahler, 47

Max Roach, 135, 206
Merriam-Webster's Collegiate Dictionary, 128
Metaphysics, 27
Microsoft Excel, 78
Microsoft OneDrive, 76
Microsoft OneNote, 78
"Mockingbirds," 31
Modern Recording Techniques, 126
"Moon River," 46
Mozart, 47, 48, 141
MS Word, 105, 148
Muhal Richard Abrams, 68, 206
MuseScore, 107, 108, 191
Music and Imagination, 127
Music Composition Analysis & Feedback (Facebook group), 58
Music Educators Journal, 143, 182, 196
Music Notation, 125, 190
Mussorgsky, 48

N
National Association for Music Education, 131, 158
National Music Camp, 60
Noteperformer, 155, 193

Notes (iPhone app), 78, 79, 136

Notion, 107, 192

O

Olympus, 22

Oontz, 108

Orchestration (by Cecil Forsyth), 126, 186

Orchestration (by Walter Piston), 126, 189

Orchestration: A Practical Handbook (by Joseph Wagner), 126, 189

Output (digital samples company), 109, 193

P

PARMA Recordings, 68, 208

Pennsylvania Angler & Boater, 175, 182, 195

"Pictures at an Exhibition," 48

Practical Vocabulary of Music in English, French, German, and Italian, 126

PRO (performance rights organization), 170

Procrastination, 39-45, 62, 122

R

Rachmaninoff, 49

Rich Matteson, 106

Rítmica, 127

Robert Gauldin, 104

Rodgers & Hammerstein, 48

S

"Sanctus," 31-32, 158

"Seophonic Rhapsody," 31

Sibelius, 23, 75, 107, 108, 109, 114, 155, 192, 205

Simple Recording, 21

Six Ps, 36

SOCAN, 79, 204, 207

Speech (Mac feature), 113

Spitfire Audio, 109, 193

Stickies, 33

Sul Ross State University, 71 141

T

Tchaikovsky, 49

Temperament, 27

"Terpsichore's Dance," 72

The Art of Dramatic Writing, 127

The Associated Press Stylebook, 112, 128

"The Bum Won," 48

The Chicago Manual of Style, 112, 128

The Complete Idiot's Guide to Music Theory, 126

The Doubleday Roget's Thesaurus in Dictionary Form, 128

The Elements of Style, 112, 128

The Harvard Dictionary of Music, 125, 190

The Instrumentalist, 143, 182, 196

"The Music Man," 48

The Shaping Forces of Music, 127

The Situation and the Story: The Art of Personal Narrative, 127

The Study of Orchestration, 125, 189

The Synonym Finder, 128

Themes and Conclusions, 127

Thomas Schudel, 67

Timaeus, 27

Tonal Composers (Facebook group), 58, 191

Treatise on Counterpoint and Fugue, 125

TRN Music Publishers, 85

Twentieth Century Harmony, 125, 188

"Two Trillion Triplets," 34, 72

V

voice memos, 21, 24, 103, 136, 174

W

WASBE, 79

Webster's New Collegiate Dictionary, 128

Western Digital My Passport, 76

"Will I Ever Tell You," 48

Windows Movie Maker (WMM), 148-149

Y

YouTube, 17, 23, 28, 53, 70, 79, 103, 116, 118, 121, 126, 129, 134, 138, 140-142, 144-149, 179, 197, 202

Z

ZenDesk+Evernote, 79

Zone and Hizohi, 67

Printed in Great Britain
by Amazon

12391573R00123